I read *Still Laughing* in one long and enjoyable sitting in front of the fireplace on an unseasonably cold day. Bill Chadwick is one fine storyteller; I laughed aloud and shed a tear or two as well. This book warmed my heart and quickened so many memories. Time and again, I nodded my head as I read and said to myself, "Just so, just so." As one might surmise, its pages are also full of potential sermon material!

> —Rev. Michael Lindvall, former pastor of Brick Presbyterian Church, New York City, and best-selling author of numerous books, including the North Haven series, *The Geography of God* and *What Did Jesus Do?*

Bill has a great gift for telling stories. At times, I couldn't stop laughing. Other times, I wept. A life-changing book, *Still Laughing* helps us see the absurdities of life and also the deep meaning of it.

> —Jolene L. Roehlkepartain, founding editor of *Children's Ministry* magazine and author of 33 books, including *Nurturing Faith in Families, Teaching Kids to Care & Share,* and *101 Great Games for Kids*

A wise rabbi once said, "God made humanity because God loves stories." There is much for God to love in Bill's stories, for they beautifully illuminate the holy in the midst of the ordinary. There is much for people like you and me to love as well, for through Bill's insight, humor and grace, something of what it means to be human is revealed, and we clearly see how our lives fit into God's greater story. A wonderful read!

> —Rev. Paul E. Gilmore, Pastor, Winnetka Presbyterian Church, Winnetka, Illinois

In *Still Laughing, Still Learning,* Pastor Bill Chadwick touches the depths of our souls while striking our funny bones squarely. He is one of the finest preachers I have ever heard, and this book captures his witty, prophetic style masterfully.

> —Jim Moline, PhD, best-selling author, executive coach, professor, theologian, and psychologist

Still Laughing,
Still Learning

(Still Looking for a Good Title)

Mostly True Stories

of

Family, Friends, Faith & Foibles

Bill Chadwick

BEAVER'S POND
PRESS

Cover Photo by Margie O'Loughlin
Book design and typesetting by Jim Handrigan
Managing Editor: Laurie Buss Herrmann

ISBN 13: 978-1-64343-889-4
Library of Congress Catalog Number: 2019914071
Printed in the United States of America
First Printing: 2020
24 23 22 21 20   5 4 3 2 1

BEAVER'S POND
PRESS

Beaver's Pond Press
939 Seventh Street West
Saint Paul, MN 55102
(952) 829-8818
www.BeaversPondPress.com

To order, visit www.ItascaBooks.com
or call (800) 901-3480 ext. 118. Reseller discounts available.
Contact the author at www.billchadwick.com for school visits, speaking engagements, book club discussions, and interviews.

To my beloveds:
Kris, Andy, Allie, Anji
(and Ruby the Wonder Dog)

CONTENTS

FOREWORD BY KEVIN KLING ix

PREFACE. xi

PRELUDE: THE CHRISTMAS EVE SERMON
The Christmas Eve Sermon 3

CHECKING CORN AND OTHER STORIES
A Heart's Desire 13
The Report Card. 20
Checking Corn. 25
A Farmer's Son 31
Remembering Hank 36
On Grace. 40

LIFE LESSONS FROM OUR ELDERS
Introduction to Chaplaincy 49
On Being Santa. 51
On Ministry in Memory Care 55
Deathbed Vigil 59
Ghosts in the Care Center?. 62
On Death. 65
On Funerals 70
On War 74
On Old Age. 77
On Baldness 82
Holy Fools 85

WOULD WE DO IT AGAIN?
On Marriage 91
I Guess We Made Our Point. 99
The Encouraging Spouse. 100
On Luck. 103

On Being a Boy. 107

On Time. 117

On Unconditional Love. 123

On Adoption. 126

Our Middle Child 136

Would We Do It Again? 139

On Being Faithful

On Humility. 149

On Reading. 151

The 3 Percent. 152

On Fun. 158

The Presence. 163

On Anger. 166

On Being a "Christian". 169

On Prognostication 172

On Listening. 177

Most Memorable Sermon. 181

Sharing a Scar. 183

On Heroes. 187

The Green Van 193

High School Class Reunions 197

On Motorcycles 201

To Know the Whole Story 204

Acknowledgments. 211

FOREWORD BY KEVIN KLING

Our earliest storytellers conjured creation stories using the landscape to teach how fire was born, why birds have particular colors, how the chipmunk got her stripes. These creatures and landscapes were familiar to everyone in the group, so to use them as conduits to the beyond aligned everyone to the pantheon of the greatest mysteries. These stories weren't meant to explain but rather to place us within creation.

I am among the Sunday morning congregation at Oak Grove Presbyterian Church, where my friend Bill Chadwick is the pastor. Early in the service, there are the general announcements—the whereabouts for the next choir practice, activities available for teens, updates on the committee being formed to furnish an apartment for a refugee family arriving on Monday. The church is full and there is a true feeling of community. After the first anthem, Bill asks the kids to come up to the front. They sit on the floor and are then introduced to "Gramps," his ventriloquist alter ego.

As Bill tells us the first part of a story, the kids focus on him, and then, when he speaks as Gramps, they shift their gaze to Gramps. (We see what we believe.) There is a lot of laughter. At first, the adults are laughing at the laughing kids, and then they are laughing at the same thing as the kids.

I'm reminded how humor connects us. Humor is not universal; it's based on a shared sense of family, faith, and community. When we laugh together, we are family, joined by what makes us human.

Bill's stories find resiliency in a collective consciousness, in belonging. Through his encounters with parishioners, family members, and total strangers, we discover that vulnerability leads to compassion and kindness, a place of grace. He understands that grace can be less a touch with the divine and more a recognition of the divine in the everyday, in finding the solace in the mystery when it seems there is no lamp to follow.

And as with the best teachers, doctors, and pastors, Bill's personal healing is tied to our own. He is on the journey with us.

The author Vladimir Nabokov believed a great story should educate, entertain, and enchant. The last of these, to enchant, refers to the ability to transport the listener or reader to a place beyond the realm and confinement of reality. A sacred space, a space that allows each of us to reach beyond our grasp. Stories of faith have always been the bridge that allows us to let go of one hand in the dark to reach for another.

In the yearly celebration of the birth of Jesus, we are told that three wise men, or kings, came from Arabia in the east, following a star. Travelers were just beginning to use the stars to navigate, hence the wise men. They came bearing gifts, and there is often speculation as to why they chose the offerings they did for the new messiah. Gold, obviously, for wealth, but why were frankincense and myrrh meaningful gifts? For one thing, they were preservatives and very useful before refrigeration. They also had analgesic, anti-inflammatory, and antiseptic properties and were prescribed for everything from hemorrhoids to halitosis. They were also frequently used in embalming. The wise men knew Jesus. "You are human now, and it's no heavenly choirs of angels down here. You are now prone to disease, infection, and bad breath—and one day even this form will cease to serve you. Here are some gifts to ease your journey."

A good gift is given with love and can be a means to return home, a bit of well-timed advice, nourishment for stomach or soul. But a great gift is an answer waiting for its question. Knowledge is acquired; wisdom is recognized.

And each of Bill's stories is just such a gift.

PREFACE

The last thing the world needs is another book.

However, the world can never have too many stories. As Philip Pullman writes, "After nourishment, shelter and companionship, stories are the thing we need most in the world."

Early in my preaching career, I used to worry about smooth transitions and clever structures for my sermons. But quickly I realized that what people are going to remember—if anything— are the stories. My motto became, "Just give them a nugget." One story for the listeners to take with them.

That's what Jesus did.

Or at least, that's what we mostly have recorded for us in the Gospels. A bunch of stories. My theory is that Jesus probably said a lot of other stuff—great propositional truths and the like—but the only things people remembered, and ultimately wrote down, were the stories.

So, I share with you some stories.

PRELUDE:

the

CHRISTMAS EVE SERMON

THE CHRISTMAS EVE SERMON

There were only two wise men left.
I sat slumped back in my chair, far from the typewriter, arms crossed, legs outstretched: the universal body language for writer's block. I gazed out the window of my second-floor study onto the scene below. A fresh blanket of snow covered some of the shabbiness of the ancient plaster-of-Paris crèche set arranged in the side yard of the church. About half life-size, the Nativity scene contained the usual cast of characters: a Baby Jesus in the manger; a seated Mary in her traditional blue dress; a nondescript Joseph standing stoically in the background; a few shepherds scattered about the edges, in the standing room–only section; and a pair of wise men in royal regalia, kneeling close in adoration. A rough-hewn wooden backdrop framed the scene, and a mature elm cast an avuncular arm over the entire tableau.

Six inches of feather-light snow sparkling in the morning sunlight would normally fill me with joy, both for its innate beauty and for the anticipation of gliding through it on cross-country skis. But there'd be no skiing and certainly no joy until I got my

Christmas Eve sermon written. It was December 22. On Sunday afternoon, the deacons had festooned the sanctuary with aromatic pine boughs and placed ribboned candles on the sill of each stained glass window. Yesterday the church office manager had typed up the worship service and run off 250 copies of the thick, carol-laden bulletin, on its cover a Nativity scene in muted colors. Last evening the choir director had put the small but faithful choir through its final rehearsals, with our new soprano ready to thrill us with "O Holy Night." Everyone was prepared.

Except the preacher . . .

I wondered how long the church had owned this crèche set. Nobody I'd talked to could remember a time before its existence. The figures were all covered with webworks of cracks, scuffs, and chips. When the deacons had hauled them out of storage at the beginning of this December, they'd determined that one of the wise men, the one in the red robe, was simply too damaged to be repaired one more time. He had succumbed to the effects of decades of silent vigil in Minnesota winters. A gaping hole had somehow been punched in his backside, and his left arm had come off. Even copious amounts of duct tape failed to secure it. The deacons had no choice but to retire him.

Since the Nativity scene was set back about thirty feet from the road—precisely to hide its condition—the deacons had decided that the rest of the crèche set was still "good enough" for now. The church members who were frantically searching for a new figure to replace the dearly departed wise man were having no success.

This did not break my heart. Despite being a pastor—okay, *because* of being a pastor—I have never been crazy about outdoor Nativity scenes. Here in Minnesota, the live ones are simply ridiculous—and thankfully rare—because the costumes never fully conceal the snowmobile suits underneath. And the still-life scenes have always seemed too reverential, too antiseptic, and . . . well, *still* to accurately depict what must have been earthy, chaotic, and confusing. Birth is exciting and loud and messy. Throw in the dazzle of some terrifying angels (every time an angel shows up in the Bible, the first thing he has to say is, "Don't be afraid!") and a few scruffy, smelly shepherds . . . then add some weird astrologers from a strange, far-off land bringing bizarre gifts that were, in fact, symbols of tribute as a vassal might bring to a king . . . toss in assorted goats, chickens, donkeys, cows . . . top it all off with a heavenly lighthouse beam showing the way and you've got quite a party! My problem with typical Nativity scenes is they offer a sense of the original events about as well as a postcard does justice to Mardi Gras.

Take into account the deteriorating condition of this particular crèche, and the irritating fact that the figures had Norwegian complexions, and I was not a big fan. But nobody asked my opinion, and so I kept it to myself.

I wondered if Nativity scenes aren't always attempting the impossible, anyway. Incarnation is such a sweet mystery: the idea that God—God!—was somehow embodied in a baby born long ago in Bethlehem. How can anything do justice to that?

Precisely my problem.

As a pastor, I had always found the "High Holy Days" of Christmas and Easter to be the hardest to preach. Everyone knows the stories so well. What can one say that is fresh and insightful?

And brief? For it's a daunting crowd on Christmas Eve. The early service, four o'clock, is full of antsy children who understandably can't wait to get home and open presents. At the ten o'clock candlelight service, it's pretty much all adults. They have just finished a monthlong marathon of buying and baking and bustling, of wrapping and writing and wrangling, of hosting and toasting and Christmas card–posting . . . a monthlong marathon run at the pace of a sixty-yard dash. Now it's Christmas Eve, and people truly *want* to be attentive and worshipful. But on top of the last month's frenzied schedule, this evening they have consumed great quantities of food and, many of them, a libation or three. The sanctuary lights are low. The candles give off a drowsy scent. Forget moving or inspiring anyone; it's a struggle just to keep them from snoring.

This was the challenge facing me. Fifty-four hours to go and I was desperate to think of something new to say.

I was drawing a blank.

It occurred to me, not for the first time, that Christmas is not about words. In fact, God chose to become flesh precisely because words didn't cut it. For centuries, prophets and teachers had tried to tell people what God was like, using words like *righteousness*, *compassion*, and *justice*. But the people didn't get it. They needed to be *shown*. And so that Bethlehem baby—born in a stable, cradled in a feedbox—grew to be a special man, a person whom many people understood to be the very incarnation of God's grace and love. Yes, Jesus talked about God with words. But he also, in some mysterious way, embodied God.

Still, the congregation would be expecting a sermon. In words.

Looking down on the Nativity scene, I tried to imagine myself joining that first motley collection of worshippers. If I were to journey to the manger, what symbol of love would I bring to the Christ Child? What eloquent words of adoration would I utter? Perhaps such an exercise would jump-start my brain . . .

Or not.

Minutes passed. I took off my glasses, rubbed my eyes, and massaged my temples. When I opened my eyes, I spotted a lone pedestrian coming down the main street sidewalk. That sidewalk was the city's responsibility, and it had not yet been cleared of the snow that fell the previous night. As I replaced my glasses, the figure came into focus. With a jolt of recognition, I leaned sideways for a better view around the leafless birch shivering outside my window.

Woolen pants, several layers of grimy woolen sweaters, woolen stocking cap, woolen gloves, a long woolen scarf trailing behind him. All drab brown and olive. A complexion that epitomized the word *swarthy*. A bit on the short side, but with the neck and shoulders of a prizefighter, and carrying a billy club. He shuffled in a semi-jog through the snow.

Buster!

I was delighted to see him, I realized with amazement—delighted from the security of my second-floor study. It had been years since I last spotted him around town. I was grateful now to discover he was still alive and out and about.

The first time I had seen him, shortly after I moved to town a dozen years earlier, I was driving near our little downtown. He was jogging along the sidewalk in an irregular sort of shuffling, forward-leaning gait. Wearing nearly the identical getup he had on today—woolen pants, sweaters, and cap.

But it wasn't December then; it was August.

Not one of those surprisingly cool late August evenings, either, but a typical August noonday: eighty-eight degrees and humid. In all that wool. He was talking loudly to himself, continually swiveling his head and looking around, jogging backward and sideways to take in his surroundings and, not infrequently, to scowl and yell at people passing by. He also shook his nightstick at them.

After that, I would see him once or twice a year, always jogging along the downtown sidewalks, always in the same attire, and always carrying the club.

In talking with folks around town, I learned a little about this man for whom life seemed so tortured. Buster hadn't been born with a problem but had lived a perfectly normal childhood, starring in sports. Turns out my first impression had been right. Not only was he built like a prizefighter; he had, in fact, been one. And that was his problem now: his brain had been injured, and he was permanently "punch-drunk."

I had great compassion for this poor soul. I'm not ashamed to say I was also very grateful I had encountered him while in the safety of my car.

Now here he was in that familiar shuffle-jog, plowing a meandering furrow through the half-foot of fluffy snow. He hadn't changed a bit in the last several years.

I was glad for the distraction. For a moment, I forgot about my sermon entirely and just watched him. As usual, Buster was muttering to himself and swiveling his body to take in everything around him—a passing pickup, the new redbrick city hall building across the street, a flock of sparrows chittering past, our quaint stone church building.

Then he spotted the crèche figures. The Holy Family in aging plaster of Paris. He veered off the sidewalk and started tromping through the snow toward them, gripping his billy club in his right hand.

I sucked air audibly through my teeth and bit my lower lip. Leaning so close to the window that I felt the cold on my forehead—my breath would have fogged the pane had I remembered to breathe—I silently pleaded, "Buster—don't touch anything!" As much as I disliked that crèche set, I realized I hated the thought of it being attacked. It had a lot of problems, but it was still a symbol of holiness.

As Buster neared the Nativity scene, his pace slowed. He almost tiptoed the last few steps. Then he stopped, front and center. He turned his head slowly to look from one figure to another—a smattering of shepherds . . . two wise men . . . Joseph . . . Mary . . . this little congregation, with all its scrapes and dents, gathering around the central mystery of our faith. All of them so vulnerable and exposed.

Buster dropped to his knees. He set down his club, removed his gloves. Gently, oh so gently, with his bare fingers, he brushed the snow off the baby Jesus.

I took a deep breath in and out. My shoulders relaxed. I swallowed and leaned back, away from the window.

There was my sermon. Almost all my parishioners knew Buster. Knew him in the same superficial way I had known him, until a few moments ago. They had watched him from the safety of their cars or homes. Felt sorry for him; feared him.

I would simply tell our parishioners what I had just witnessed. Show them the story of Love Incarnate.

The third wise man had arrived.

CHECKING CORN

and

OTHER STORIES

A HEART'S DESIRE

I lay on my belly in the living room, making out my combined birthday/Christmas list. Next to me on the gold carpet was the Montgomery Ward catalog, my reference book. Mom had stacked LPs on the turntable of our giant stereo/radio/television console, and Bing, Perry, and Andy were softly crooning the season's first carols. Goldfinches flitted on the feeder outside (when the squirrels would allow them near).

From frequent perusal, the fat, shiny-paged "Monkey Ward" catalog now opened automatically to the toy section. Page after page of baseballs and basketballs, tennis rackets and toy rockets, Erector sets and chemistry sets, microscopes and telescopes. But I had eyes for only one thing. And there it was, staring up at me from page 356.

A Daisy pump-action BB gun.

I would gladly forgo all other presents if I could just have a BB gun!

Was it because every Sunday evening my brother and I plopped ourselves down in front of that black-and-white TV to watch Fess Parker as Davy Crockett respond to the threat-of-the-week—whether wild animals or wild men—with his trusty rifle?

Or was it because I was an avid reader, especially enjoying biographies of explorers of the American frontier? Men like Kit Carson and Jim Bridger filled my imagination. I was thrilled to share a name with Wild Bill Hickok and Buffalo Bill Cody.

In the lives of all of these larger-than-life heroes, guns played a central role. Hungry? Shoot something. Somebody bothering you? Shoot him.

In my own world, my father watched the six o'clock news each evening on television and I learned that a US spy plane had been shot down over Russia. Followed by the Bay of Pigs invasion. Civil defense raids in school, as we hid under our desks. The Cuban Missile Crisis.

Sputnik sliding across the evening sky. I watched, mesmerized.

The Moscow May Day parade each year featured Soviet soldiers marching across Red Square by the thousands, rank upon rank followed by tank upon tank.

I played with my little green plastic army men; our neighbors built a bomb shelter.

I don't know for sure if any of these fantasies—or realities—fueled my desire. I don't recall wanting to actually shoot somebody. I do know that, for whatever reason, I longed, I yearned, I *ached* for a BB gun in a way I had never longed for anything else.

All I had to do was to convince my parents I could be trusted with a gun. I was nine.

My parents said no in precisely the same way Ralphie's would respond in *A Christmas Story* twenty years later: "You'll shoot somebody's eye out."

Carefully reasoned arguments did no good:

"I'll use my own money."

"I'm almost *ten* years old."

"I'll be *caaaaaaarrrreful!*"

I couldn't use the usual ploy of "everybody else has one" because no one I knew did. And that would make my owning a BB gun all the sweeter!

Relentless pleading did no good, even with my dad—dear old, softhearted Dad. "You're not getting a BB gun. What if you shoot somebody's eye out?"

I was diligent in my efforts to show I was responsible, taking out the garbage without being reminded—more than two or three times. I was tireless in my begging.

My parents did not show the slightest signs of cracking under the pressure, and their refusals sounded convincing. However, I thought back to an incident from a few years earlier. About a week before Christmas, I had discovered a huge container of Lincoln Logs in a corner of the garage and excitedly asked, "Are they for me?" Without the slightest hesitation, my mother told me they were for my cousin David, and we were just hiding them here until Christmas. I was deeply disappointed, but I fully accepted that very plausible explanation. When I unwrapped a large package on Christmas morning, I was overjoyed to discover it was the Lincoln Logs. For me!

I was also astonished. Astounded. Dumbfounded.

In our family, honesty was held up as the highest possible value, its importance emphasized repeatedly and firmly throughout our childhoods. Yet my mother had lied to me with a perfectly straight face, as cool and calm as any Cold War spy.

What else might she be capable of? Our relationship changed at the moment of my unwrapping the Lincoln Logs.

So, despite my parents' firm denials, I still held out hope that maybe I *would* get a BB gun.

I didn't get a BB gun for my birthday, December 10.

I didn't get a BB gun for Christmas . . . sigh.

I resigned myself to waiting until I went to college. Then I'd buy my *own* BB gun. I tried my best to put it out of my mind.

But a few months later, while our family was visiting my great-uncle Guy and great-aunt Liddy, who lived nearby, Uncle Guy called me out to the garage. There, he unceremoniously handed me a BB gun rifle and said, "I never use it anymore. You can have it if you'd like."

I stood there, paralyzed. I blinked a few times. I was holding a BB gun.

If I'd like? *If I'd like!*

I hadn't even known Uncle Guy owned a BB gun. Never before and never in the fifty years since have I been so stupefied. When I could speak, I croaked, "This is for me?"

"Yes."

"To keep?"

"Yes."

"It's *mine* now?"

"Yes! Yours now. Don't shoot anybody's eye out."

Wonder of wonders! Miracle of miracles!

I'm certain the gift was bestowed without the prior knowledge of my parents. The true wonder was that my parents let me keep it. In fact, they allowed me to use it pretty much whenever I wanted. As a parent now myself, I can only shake my head in utter Dr. Phil perplexity: "*What* were they thinking?"

I can excuse my great-uncle because he was very old at the time and, more importantly, he had never had children. He didn't know the potential ramifications of arming a ten-year-old boy.

At any rate, I was now the proud owner—no, *proud* doesn't do it justice—I was the *incredulously ecstatic* owner of my very own BB gun. It wasn't a new pump-action Daisy. In fact, it must have been very, very old, going by the style and by the countless scratches on the real wooden stock, and even on the metal barrel.

But it worked! A real gun!

Immediately, I was the envy of all the neighborhood boys, even the ones four or five years older than I.

Well. What to shoot?

Squirrels were the logical choice. We lived on a one-acre lot with dozens of oak trees. We had oodles of gray squirrels. And they ate all the sunflower seeds out of the feeder and scared the birds away. Certainly my parents would not only allow me to shoot squirrels but thank me for it.

I'm quite sure I didn't actually ask.

So. A-hunting I would go, usually with some extremely envious friend tagging along and begging for a turn, which I would, from time to time, magnanimously grant.

Either we weren't good shots or the rifle didn't fire very true—possibly both—but we went weeks without hitting any target smaller than a mature oak tree. Then one day I took careful aim at the side of a plump gray squirrel in a tree about twenty-five feet away. I slowly pulled the trigger and . . . bull's-eye!

The squirrel and I were equally surprised. I was also baffled when the BB bounced off his side and he scurried away unharmed.

What a disappointment. Clearly, I needed a bigger gun.

Or smaller game.

One day late that summer, a group of kids gathered in our front yard. The crowd included some older boys who had just finished working for the day on my dad's farm. I cradled my gun nonchalantly. The oldest boy, about seventeen or eighteen, asked to see it. Wow! A teenager acknowledging my existence. The magical power of a gun.

I handed it over. In the boy's long arms, it looked more like a toy than a real gun. He inspected its worn stock and scratched barrel. We could hear the BBs rolling around inside. Looking around for a target in the universal way of boys, he finally spotted one almost directly overhead. Perched on the tip of a branch about ten or twelve feet above him was a large monarch butterfly, regally sunning its wings.

"Think I can shoot its head off?"

A sarcastic chorus of "Yeah, right," "I'm sure," and "In your dreams!" rose from the circle of boys.

The teenager took a seat on the grass. He raised the rifle to aim almost directly overhead at the butterfly.

Vivid orange with velvety black spots, almost glistening in the sunlight, the butterfly slowly closed its wings and opened them again. It did not leave its perch. Its head was almost precisely the size of a BB.

The boy took a long time aiming. The air was still. The cluster of boys was motionless and silent. All of them were concentrating as intently as the shooter.

I had time to consider a whirlwind of thoughts. Monarchs had always been my favorite of all the creatures in our yard. The previous summer I had found a monarch caterpillar and put it in a mason jar with some leaves and twigs. I watched the caterpillar attach itself to a twig and then hang down. It fashioned a chrysalis from the bottom up, and I waited impatiently. After two weeks, the slightest of movements. Then a tiny hole appeared at the bottom. Over the course of hours, the creature struggled its way free. Still clinging to the chrysalis, it slowly moved its wings back and forth to dry them. When finally it began to flutter around the jar, I released it and watched with joy and pride as it flew away into the sunlight and disappeared into the trees. What a dramatic transformation! From a lowly caterpillar oonching its way along a tree branch into a delicate creature of transcendent beauty and magical flight.

So I strongly didn't want the teenager to kill this butterfly. But I couldn't say anything. The other kids would have made fun of me. "Oh well," I thought. "There's absolutely no chance he'll hit it anyhow."

I suppose, as I reflect on it now, that maybe similar thoughts were going through the other boys' heads. Perhaps even the shooter's, for he took forever. Aiming. Aiming. One eye closed.

None of us said a word. We were gazing up intently at the butterfly.

Finally, the boy gently squeezed the trigger. A soft "tew" sound.

The monarch tumbled off the branch and zigzagged to the ground.

Headless.

With shouts of amazement and admiration, the other boys rushed to gaze for a moment at the still form of the butterfly. Then they boisterously clapped the shooter on the back, congratulating him for his truly remarkable shot.

I stared at the lifeless monarch.

The boy got up from his seat, strode over to me, and handed back my gun.

I hesitated; then, without looking up at him, I took it back reluctantly. I didn't say a word.

Soon the boys scattered. I sat there with my mouth dry, my throat tight, not looking at the butterfly condemning me silently from where it lay in the grass.

I looked at the gun in my lap. I hadn't shot another kid in the eye. That was something.

But still I felt a little betrayed. Why hadn't my parents protected me from this? Why had they given in? Had they decided that what their tenderhearted kid might learn with that ratty old gun was worth the risk?

I never used the BB gun after that. I don't even know what happened to it.

Years later I was to learn that in the ancient Church, the butterfly was a symbol of the Resurrection. Today I own a liturgical stole covered in butterflies, which I wear at memorial services.

THE REPORT CARD

I was good at school.

That is, I got good grades. Other kids were good at sports or were confident in social situations. And believe you me, most days I would have traded my grades for either of those other two things.

Everybody's good at something. For the most part, the academic side of school came easy for me—which was fortunate, because my parents had high expectations. You see, my older brother was perfect. No, wait. My mistake. He did receive one B+ in his entire high school career, which dropped him down to seventh in his class of four hundred students. That "seventh in his class of four hundred" was my mother's mantra, her standard response to any of my complaints about homework.

Simply put, my parents expected excellent grades: "You're a Chadwick."

I came through. In junior high, the first time we were given actual letter grades, I came home with a roughly equal number of As and Bs—Bs in phys ed and art; As in math, science, and English.

In ninth grade, my last year of junior high, I discovered girls.

Well, actually, I had discovered them years earlier in the sense of noticing their existence *and* finding them intriguing. But it wasn't until about the middle of ninth grade that I also found the ability to open my mouth and make an actual utterance in their presence.

And I learned that one of them, a girl I'd had a tremendous crush on since fourth grade, actually liked me back!

Wonder of wonders! Miracle of miracles!

Of course, discovering we liked each other wasn't as easy as I just made it sound. Gaining such knowledge required weeks and weeks of whispering and note passing.

Not between us. Of course not!

Between our mutual friends.

At any rate, the truth eventually became clear; and suddenly, academics no longer seemed so all-fired important.

Coincidentally—providentially, I thought—in my ninth-grade year, our school introduced an experimental scheduling system in which we no longer had six one-hour classes each day. Instead, we had modular scheduling, similar to college in that it included a whole lot of free time. The theory was that during all this free time, we'd go to various study areas and do our assignments. Though if we felt we "needed a break," we could also go down to the cafeteria and visit with our friends for a while.

Right. This was junior high. Can you imagine? Of course, it was the 1960s . . .

For the first half of the year, I was one of eleven total nerds who actually did use the free time to complete assignments and study for tests. I did this for two reasons: firstly, I had to walk a mile to and from school, and so the fewer books I had to carry for homework, the better; secondly, I was far too bashful to use that free time in any constructive way, like to talk to a girl or something.

But midway through ninth grade, something happened. Evidently, enough testosterone started pumping through my system to overwhelm whatever scrap of genetic material or misfiring neuron had been responsible for my natural shyness. Actually, a number of people noted how almost overnight I metamorphosed from extremely introverted to extremely obnoxious.

Again, I blame it on hormones.

No, scratch that. I *credit* it to hormones. Anything, even obnoxiousness, was preferable to my experience of shyness (though the pimples I could have done without).

Suddenly, I was the one flinging kids off the side of the hayride wagon; I was the one making dumb jokes at parties instead of sitting silently in the corner. I knew I had really made it from the total nerd side of the social strata to the tolerably cool side when some of the other track guys put Ben-Gay in my underwear while I was in the shower. (I know it sounds like picking on the nerd, but in our school, the cool guys played this nasty trick only on one another. So I was thrilled. Painfully thrilled, but thrilled nonetheless.)

Third quarter, I spent a lot of time not in the study areas but in the cafeteria. Previously, I had focused on deciphering algebraic formulas, diagramming sentences, and memorizing Spanish vocab (*cordero,* "lamb"—think "corduroy lamb"). But all of these receded in importance when put up against the lure of talking to a girl, occasionally even holding her hand!

Whoa!

Cordero . . . lamb . . . "Ahh," I thought, "my little lamb . . ."

I had it bad.

I'll admit I was a tad worried about how this new use of my time might affect my grades. But hey, I was always a good test-taker. And with my newfound confidence, maybe I could bluff my way through some essay tests. At any rate, finals were a loooong way off.

Her smile at the sight of me coming down the hallway left me weak-kneed and incredulous. We held hands as we walked the corridors of the school. Her hand was so delicate and soft . . . oh, my.

We met at each other's lockers. We talked on the phone. I went to her dance recital. She laughed at my jokes. On weekends at our friends' parties, we slow-danced in the basement. After six or seven weeks of this courtship, we actually . . . kissed.

Sort of.

I shut my eyes too soon and kind of caught her on the side of the nose. But she adjusted, and for a few sweet seconds, our lips brushed.

I didn't mind her braces.

A couple of months into this romance, third-quarter grades came out. My report card included some As, some Bs, and . . . a C. In fact, not one C but *two*.

My parents had never once encountered a C, from either of their sons. "Well, this ought to be interesting," I thought as I set the report card out on the counter for my parents to see when they came home. I didn't know exactly how they would respond. We had entered uncharted seas.

I knew my parents weren't going to whip me or even yell at me. But I also knew they were going to be *very* disappointed. I felt horrible about that. I headed up to my bedroom, figuring it wouldn't hurt if they found me studying at my desk when they came home.

Some time later, I heard the two of them having a quiet conversation downstairs. Hoo boy, I wondered what it would be . . . Grounded? No TV for a while?

Soon I sensed my father's heavy footfalls on the stairs. A knock on my door.

"Come in." I tried to say it offhandedly, as if nothing were out of the ordinary. But my voice cracked (of course), and I had to clear my throat and say it again.

My dad sat down on the bed. For a moment, he looked at his hands folded in his lap. With a thoughtful expression, he raised his gaze and stated flatly, "We saw your report card." I nodded.

Getting no verbal response, he continued. "Your mother thought that I should talk to you about those Cs."

I nodded again.

"But I'm not going to. I just want to congratulate you on the As and Bs."

He rose from the bed, put his hand on my shoulder for a second . . . and, that utterly gracious man, left the room.

I never got another C.

And I married the girl.

CHECKING CORN

My mother started calling me "the absentminded professor" when I was only seven or eight years old. Most boys are not good at remembering things—to take out the garbage, to put dirty clothes in the hamper, to bring signed permission slips back to the teacher. But I brought forgetting to new heights. I was an artist. Unmatched. First-class. Blue-ribbon. When I was eighteen, I forgot to file my student deferment for the draft.

When the Vietnam War was just beginning to ramp up, I was in junior high. Given my unpleasant early experience with a BB gun, I wasn't enamored with the idea of killing. But I did view the conflict as my chance to join that long line of heroes who had fought for our country, for democracy. Those TV ads were so compelling: "The Few. The Proud. The Marines." What adolescent boy could resist?

In an eighth-grade social studies class discussion about the war, I declared my intention to go fight. That is, if the war was still going on in four years, when I graduated. But we all agreed this was highly unlikely. The president and his generals weekly assured the public that we were winning and it would all be over soon.

But if not, I was in! Signing up would require a signature from at least one of my parents, since I would only be seventeen at graduation, but what parent wouldn't want their son to be a hero?

Day after day, the conflict continued.

Month after month. Year after year, the killing and the dying went on.

It was the first televised war in American history. The evening news showed flag-draped coffins coming off the transport planes each day by the dozens, sometimes by the hundreds. (In our more recent conflicts, the US government has chosen to prevent those images from reaching us. They tend to diminish the public's enthusiasm for war.) The death-toll figures were reported each night like the stock-exchange numbers: "Thirty-seven US soldiers reported killed in Vietnam today . . . This week, over two hundred Americans killed or wounded . . ."

As the fighting marched on, the draft resisters began to march as well. Even a sixteen-year-old could begin to see this war was not like World War II. Was it accomplishing anything worthwhile?

By the time I graduated from high school, I had changed my mind about participating in this conflict. I said to myself and others that had it been something like a response to the attack on Pearl Harbor, I'd be the first in line at the recruiting station. But this seemed like a mess we shouldn't have gotten into in the first place. (Obviously, I wasn't alone in this assessment.)

The My Lai Massacre and the shooting of students at Kent State further diminished my enthusiasm for the entire war effort.

So off I went to college. Among the many forms we incoming freshmen boys filled out in those first few days of orientation was a registration for our college/student deferment from the draft. At least, you filled it out if you were eighteen, as almost all my classmates were. But my birthday wasn't until December. Not once that semester did I give it another thought.

My birthday came right in the midst of finals. In the flurry of worrying and studying, I forgot to register for the student deferment.

For months.

By the time I thought of it, it was too late. Thus, as the draft lottery for young men born in 1952 rolled around, I was not classified 2-S ("deferred because of activity in study") as I could have been; I was 1-A: available for service. Just like all the guys who were too poor to go to college or who didn't have the grades, I was prime beef for the war machine, going to Vietnam.

But only if I got a low number in the lottery.

The draft lottery was held in late summer. Weather-wise, it was a glorious day, sunny and warm but not too hot. The sort of day that happens three hundred times a year in Southern California but is rare enough in Minnesota that we savor each one.

I was working at my brother's fruit-and-vegetable market, along with about eight other young guys. Two of us—my longtime friend Brad and I—were 1-A. Two kids. Brad had just turned nineteen; I was still eighteen.

As the lottery selection began, we listened intently to the radio broadcast as we continued to check sweet corn. The point of "checking corn" is to search for corn earworms at the top of each ear. You slice between the leaves with a paring knife and peel them back a couple of inches. If there's a wormy section, it will be at the top. If an ear looked okay, we pulled the leaves back up and placed it on the table to our left. If worm damage wasn't too extensive, we cut the top off and put the ear in the stack with the others. Someone else would bag the corn into baker's dozens for sale.

Rarely, but occasionally, we would find a bulbous gray growth of fungus attached to the ear, which was called *smut*, believe it or not. Those ears went straight into the garbage.

All of us were experienced and fast corn checkers. We could do it without thinking, which meant we could concentrate on the radio.

In the lottery, birth dates were drawn from a barrel, and numbers from 1 to 366 (1952 was a leap year) were selected from a different container. Then they were matched. So over the radio, we heard:

"May 4 . . . Number 283."

"September 9 . . . Number 199."

The army would require about one-third of eligible candidates to be conscripted, so up to about number 120. If your number was above 140, you were most likely safe. Anyone below 100 would almost certainly be drafted.

If you were drafted and you passed the physical, you had four choices. Most chose to go into the military. Some young men were fleeing the country, often to Canada, not knowing if they would ever be allowed to return. You could also apply to be a conscientious objector, or you could go to jail.

I didn't believe that the US cause in Southeast Asia was just and I was unwilling to kill other human beings for it, so I was not going to go into the army. But I couldn't apply to be a conscientious objector because, at that time, I wasn't against *all* wars—just this one.

I didn't want to go to Canada and never be allowed to enter the US again, never see my family except when they came to visit. So if I got a low number, I planned to go to jail.

Who knew what I would actually do if the moment of truth came?

Brad wasn't completely certain what he would do. What he was sure of, with all his heart, was that he did *not* want to go to Vietnam.

That afternoon at the market, the two of us were excused from waiting on customers so we could focus on the radio as we checked corn. Minutes passed amid the bustle of customers at the checkout counters a few feet in front of us and supply trucks coming and going at the receiving door twenty feet behind.

From time to time, I looked over at Brad. How would each of us fare in military conflict or in jail? Brad was short but, having been a star wrestler in high school, he had no trouble throwing gunnysacks of corn around. I was of medium height and skinny to the point of scrawny.

"February 21 . . . Number 15." Ouch! Poor guys . . .

"February 24 . . . Number 215." Lucky! Oh, how I wished my birthday was February 24!

Every time our birth months were called—Brad's was May, mine December—we tensed. And then let out a sigh when they read someone else's date.

We continued to check corn. Three ears in a row, I found ears sprouting gross smut. I wondered if that was a bad omen.

Next summer, would we be checking corn on golden days like this one and going out with our girlfriends in the evening? Or would we be slogging through the swamps of Vietnam with bullets whizzing by and our friends' legs being blown off by mines? Would we be in some dim jail cell, locked away from family and friends and freedom? Or would we choose exile in Quebec or Ontario? Or . . . ?

"December . . ." We both froze.

"10." My birthday! Two seconds seemed like two months.

"Number 362."

I felt my shoulders drop and I slumped onto the table as my co-workers mobbed me with congratulations. I almost puked with relief.

But it wasn't time to celebrate yet. I quieted everyone down and glanced at Brad.

It wasn't a long wait. "May 5 . . .

"Number 41."

Brad's shoulders slumped too. His head bowed. Eyes blank. Wordlessly he set his knife down on the corn table, untied his apron and placed it next to the knife, turned on his heel, and walked out the back door of the market into the sunshine of a beautiful Minnesota day. And kept walking.

He did not come back to work that day.

That fall, I returned to college feeling very lucky.

Brad went into the army. Fortunately, he was sent to Germany rather than Vietnam.

A lot of other guys weren't so lucky.

You can see the names of 58,195 of them on a long, black wall in Washington, DC.

A Farmer's Son

I remember playing catch with my dad one day.
I remember it so distinctly because it was the only time he
ever played catch with me. I also remember him taking me to
a Minnesota Twins baseball game—once.

You might be thinking, "What a rotten dad! Was he not in the
home? Was he a drinker? Was he sick?"

The answer to all three is no. My dad didn't play catch with
me, and he didn't take me to a bunch of ball games, because he
didn't see that as his role.

At the time, I do remember wishing he would do a few more
of those "play" things with me, but don't get the wrong impression; I did not at all feel neglected. It was a different culture then.
Today, so many parents attempt to make children feel they are the
center of the universe. Parents—at least the suburban parents I
am most familiar with—do everything in their power to attend all
their kids' games and most of the practices. Many parents today
seek to be in the midst of every aspect of their kids' lives. It used to
be the other way around: kids wanted to join their *parents'* world,
which strikes me as a healthier thing. For everyone.

Instead of being my baseball buddy, what did my dad do?

I was with my dad a lot, riding along on the tractor when I was little, accompanying him in the lumbering Ford truck on deliveries of produce to various markets, sharing hamburgers and chocolate malted milks at the drugstore soda fountain. I observed his kindness to the ladies behind the counter.

While we traveled along in the truck together, Dad would regale us kids with stories. Funny stories, interesting stories about the early days of our hometown: going to school in a one-room schoolhouse, all the students reciting their lessons aloud simultaneously; hoeing a giant field of onions for eight cents an hour; looking for arrowheads down by the creek. He chuckled as he told of the time when, as a young man, he played a prank on his friend Hank. (You'll hear more about Hank later.) Hank retaliated by completely filling Dad's car with snow, the interior firmly packed to the very top.

Dad would recite poetry he had memorized in school fifty years earlier (though, like most men, he couldn't remember the three things Mom asked him to pick up at the store).

And sayings. Oh, did he have sayings . . .

> "What we call luck is simply pluck
> And doing things over and over.
> Courage and will,
> Perseverance and skill
> Are the four leaves of luck's clover."

He certainly modeled hard work: in the summertime rising at 3:30 a.m. to go to market, returning at about 9:00, working on the farm all day, and then, after supper, heading out to the shed to grade tomatoes.

Although he worked hard, he wasn't in a hurry. He regularly paused during the day to gaze at the geese flying overhead in the spring, to appreciate the symmetrical beauty of a perfect ear of sweet corn, to sniff the wild honeysuckle growing along the edges of the farm, to behold the flaming maples in the fall.

I wish I had learned this lesson better from Dad. I am so often hurrying, careening from one appointment to another, from one task to the next, symbolically out of breath much of the day. I once read, "A saint is someone who is not filled with hurry, flurry, or worry." By that definition, Dad was a saint. (By that definition, or any other, I most assuredly am not.)

He took me with him when he delivered free firewood to a poor family in our neighborhood, so they could heat their house.

One year, he sat me down next to him in his den, pulled out his big ledger book, and laid it open on his metal desk. He showed me the list—written in his small but neat handwriting—of organizations he and my mom supported financially each year. I didn't at all sense he was bragging. I knew he wanted to model generosity and compassion for me.

Speaking of Dad's den, my little brother and I were the recipients of the most fantastic gift from our older brother one year, upon his return from a college spring break trip to Florida—two live alligators, each about fifteen inches long. You could do that in those days. We put them in an aquarium left over from our tropical fish days, along with some big rocks and a few inches of water. But where to put the aquarium? We three boys shared a bedroom; full of boys, it had no room for alligators. And for some strange reason, Mom didn't want the alligators in the living room.

So they resided in Dad's den. We fed them hamburger and occasionally minnows we netted in the nearby creek. The gators ate a lot. Thus, they pooped a lot. And amazingly enough, the two of us little kids didn't clean the aquarium very often. I don't know how Dad put up with the stench as long as he did. He was a patient man.

Dad was openly affectionate with my mom. At the time, of course, it mortified me, seeing them smooching or slow-dancing in the kitchen. But I realize now what a gift that example was to us kids, an example too few kids have.

And he cried. Easily. Frequently. At sappy movies and television shows, on occasion. But always when one of us kids disappointed him or, more commonly, made him proud.

When I was a boy, the sight of this barrel-chested 200-pound farmer tearing up all the time hugely embarrassed me.

As a man, I envy his tenderness and gentleness. I wish I were more like him.

Once, in the midst of a heated church discussion about whether to build a larger sanctuary or not, he rose to his feet and, with tears in his eyes, gently asked (thirty years before the *WWJD* bracelets), "What would Jesus want us to do?"

When my siblings and I were arguing, threatening to inflict mayhem and great bodily harm on one another, Dad quietly quoted Proverbs in the King James Version: "A soft answer turneth away wrath."

One fall, Dad and I drove out to our pumpkin patch. We found a mother and her two kids carrying pumpkins toward their car parked along the roadside. When we stopped by her car, the woman apologized profusely.

Then, however, she tried to justify her actions: "But there are so many. I didn't think you would miss a few."

Dad replied, "Well, Dayton's has hundreds of dresses. You don't just take a few, do you?"

She shook her head silently.

"Well, go ahead and take the pumpkins," said my dad.

I was shocked. What was he thinking?

"Oh, I couldn't," responded the woman. "No."

"Take 'em," Dad said calmly.

"Then let me pay you for them." The woman reached into the car for her purse.

"No," he said. "I insist."

So the woman and her kids sheepishly and silently loaded the pumpkins into the car and drove away. I doubt that woman tried to steal anything from anyone ever again.

Today I see helicopter parents storming into the school principal's office when their child is caught misbehaving, sure that their little darling couldn't possibly be guilty of the alleged infraction or furious that a teacher won't raise their child's grade. If their dear child is not excelling academically, it must be the teacher's fault! For my siblings and me, there was never any question whose side my dad was going to be on if there were an issue at school. (Hint: it wasn't ours.) Needless to say, we tried really hard not to have any issues at school. It has stood us in good stead. As my younger brother says, "If parents aren't hard on a kid, life will be."

In our school system, we were given two grades in each class: an academic grade of A, B, C, D, or F, and a citizenship grade of 1, 2, or 3. Dad was very clear that working hard on homework and tests and getting good grades was important. But he said the citizenship grade was the one he cared about more—what kind of person we were, more than what kind of student.

He taught us kids to tell the truth and to do the right thing. Always. No exceptions. "I don't care what the other kids are doing. You're a Chadwick."

Since his death thirty years ago, countless people, upon learning I am Ed Chadwick's son, have told me stories about their own encounters with him: how he encouraged them, gave them jobs or second chances, or even paid the down payment on their parents' house!

On Father's Day—and every day—I'm grateful beyond words for my dad.

Remembering Hank

Our family was gathered around the dining-room table for our typical Sunday dinner of beef roast, potatoes and gravy, bread and butter, sweet corn, Jell-O, big glasses of milk, and ice cream for dessert. As usual, the entire family was there—Dad, Mom, my big brother and big sister, my little brother, and me—and, as usual, we were commenting on the morning's church service.

It was the 1960s, and the children's music director wore very short skirts while she directed with great energy. My father expressed his opinion that the skirt was inappropriate and he did not find the spectacle worshipful. My older brother, Cal, twenty-one years old, didn't say anything, but his wink in my direction indicated he thought her skirts were just fine. I was twelve and just beginning to appreciate things like that.

Cal said, "I thought the service was excellent today. Except I thought I was going to lose my cookies when Hank cleared his throat."

Hank was a farmer, like my dad, and they had been friends all their lives. Hank and Mabel lived on the same plot Hank's grandfather had homesteaded, and Hank was good at his work, especially well-known for his potatoes. Mabel worked side by side with him on the farm.

At one point they had kept a small herd of Holsteins as well, which meant milking every day at 5:00 a.m. and 5:00 p.m. Every day. Dairy cows don't take days off. Hank was famous for once having gone eleven years without missing a milking.

Hank had a round face, an easy smile, and a deep, slow chuckle. When I knew him, his black hair was thinning, his middle slowly increasing. Hank spent a lot of time in the sun, and his leathery skin was astonishingly brown year-round. Mabel was tall and slender, with bright eyes and an infectious laugh that reminded me of a stream tumbling down over the rapids.

Hank and Mabel—never *Mabel and Hank*, we thought of them as *HankandMabel*—didn't have any children or other close relatives nearby, so they spent most holidays with our family, usually in our home but sometimes at their big and old-fashioned, white two-story farmhouse. Mabel was delighted to cook for more than two, so when they had company she went all out—big slabs of meat and several kinds of potatoes as well as fresh-picked tomatoes, muskmelons, summer squash, home-baked bread, and, to top it off, two or three different kinds of pies, fresh from the oven: peach, apple, perhaps strawberry-rhubarb, with ice cream dripping off the top and down the side of each slice.

They played bridge with our parents a couple times a month and always asked us kids what we were studying in school, about the sports we played or the concerts we were in. When we spent Christmas Eve together, they always gave each of us a present— usually something useful, like socks, but hey, it's the thought that counts, and we were grateful.

HankandMabel were to me like a beloved uncle and aunt. (It was not until I was in my teens that I discovered, to my utter amazement, that they were not married as I had always assumed. They were brother and sister! But that's a story for another time.)

At church that morning, Hank had cleared his throat. It happened a time or two (or three) every Sunday, usually during the sermon: the noise rising like the growl of some weird, exotic creature coming from the rear of the sanctuary, where Hank preferred to sit. In hindsight, I wonder if the throat clearing was Hank's way of indicating to the preacher that he had missed a few good stopping places.

You see, Hank didn't just "clear his throat." This multistep procedure consisted of a sucking in and a snort, then a rumbling growl that lasted several seconds, followed by coughing and liquid swishing around in his mouth. It was a sound that if you heard it outside your tent at 2:00 a.m. while camping in the wilderness, your night of sleep would be over. And perhaps your sleeping bag would be damp. And understand that Hank made no attempt to be quiet or discreet. I've never heard anything remotely like it before or since.

So when my older brother commented on it at the dinner table, he was immediately met with a chorus of agreement:

"Oh, I know. It was the worst ever."

"It just makes me wanna puke."

"I can't stand it!"

"I bet Mabel wants to die of embarrassment."

I sat there in astonishment, looking around at each member of my family.

"Huh," I thought. "That has never grossed me out." Perhaps it helped that I was a twelve-year-old boy, and so pretty much nothing grossed me out.

To me, that sound simply meant one thing: "Hank's here."

Of course, Hank was always there. A guy who goes eleven years without missing a twice-daily milking is someone who won't find once-a-week church attendance too taxing. But it was still reassuring to hear that sound and know "Hank's here." Hank's here, in his usual spot in the back; and if there were ever any need for it, Hank would *have my back*. It gave me a warm feeling. To me, Hank's throat-clearing meant *church* as much as the organ music or the sermon; and it meant *family* and *home* as much as the clatter of dinner plates every Sunday, and my father's disapproving comments about changing fashions, and the smell of Mabel's strawberry-rhubarb pie.

I'd give anything to hear him clear his throat again.

ON GRACE

There's an old story of a little girl coloring away in Sunday School class, tongue jammed firmly in the corner of her mouth, brow furrowed in concentration.

"What are you drawing?" asked her teacher.

"God."

Thoughtful pause, then gently, "But, honey, nobody knows what God looks like."

"They will when I'm finished."

The Sunday School teacher was right: nobody knows what God looks like. Any time we attempt to speak of the Divine Mystery, we do so recognizing how inadequate all our descriptions are. We can only hint at that which is beyond comprehension and certainly beyond our words.

Nevertheless, I'll have a go: God is like my grandma.

I recognize the audacity of that statement. Let me explain.

My grandmother had twenty-one grandchildren.

I was her favorite.

In my warmest memories of Grandma, I am always about seven or eight years old. A kind of golden age, when a little independence and responsibility have put babyhood behind you but the pressures and insecurities of pre-adolescence are still distant on the horizon. One such memory comes to mind: "Boys! Boys! My blood pressure!" Grandma was scampering around the outside of a circle of swinging legs and arms, squeals and laughter—a circle made up of my three older boy cousins, ages ten to fourteen, wrestling on her living room floor, laughing and punching and tickling and kicking (though careful not to actually hurt anybody). I, being a few years younger and half their size, sat a safe distance away at the edge of Grandma's living room, horrified at my cousins' disrespect. "Boys! Boys!" Grandma continued to scold, trying to grab a whirling foot or arm to pull them apart. Utterly futile. My cousins completely ignored her pleas, which upset me. I didn't want Grandma to be distressed, because she loved us so.

"Stop now! Let's make some popcorn balls." That got their attention. Maple syrup was warmed on the stove while Grandma popped a giant bowl of popcorn. The syrup was poured all over the popcorn and then we all slathered our hands in butter and clumped the popcorn into snowball-sized balls to eat while we watched cartoons. Even more fun than wrestling.

Grandma was synonymous with *food*. She loved nothing better than to cook golden-brown turkeys, steaming mashed potatoes, sweet potato casseroles, and delectable dressings; to bake apple and pumpkin pies and chocolate cakes. And no one, but no one, produced gravy like Grandma's. The aromas wafting out of her kitchen . . . Heaven can't smell any better.

If you were looking for a midwestern grandmother, my grandma, Daisy Mae Brown, was right out of central casting— short and round, wrinkly and smiley, an apron invariably tied around her waist, and smelling of talcum powder and whatever she had just been cooking. Every Thanksgiving and Christmas Day were spent at Grandpa and Grandma's house with each of the four children, their spouses, and all twenty-one grandchildren. (Three of the four children married Roman Catholics.) Directly behind the house was the town park with an ice-skating rink, warming house, and huge sledding hill. (When I drive past now, I am astounded at how much that hill has shrunk in the intervening decades.) Between Grandma's incredible food, the exhilarating speed and heartiness of cold-weather games, and *twenty* other kids to play with, those holidays generated memories for me that are pure Norman Rockwell.

We also spent many summer days at my grandparents' cabins. Two little cabins next door to each other on a small lake "up north," a peculiarly Minnesotan term. Grandpa and Grandma would stay in one cabin, and their four adult kids and their families would come up, one family at a time, to stay in the other. Each morning Grandma was the first one up. Breakfast was steaming pancakes or waffles, sizzling bacon and sausage, warm blueberry muffins slathered in butter. All made from scratch. Lunch might only be sandwiches and potato salad. But supper? Some combination of fried fish, homemade soup and rolls, hamburgers, baked chicken, corn on the cob dripping in butter . . . Company tended to drop in right at mealtime.

After supper, a few of us would clamber into Grandpa's fourteen-foot aluminum fishing boat with the white Johnson three-horse outboard motor and begin putt-putting slowly around the lake. (Grandma didn't participate. She couldn't swim, and she didn't like to touch fish until they had been turned into fillets.) We trolled nothing but identical green Lazy Ike lures, catching many weeds—"Irish bass," my grandpa called them—and usually a few modest northern pike, mostly hammer handle–sized. When the sunset turned from orange to red to purple, and darkness settled over the lake, the loons would begin their maniacal calls and the mosquitoes would drive us inside, banging the screen door behind us. (To be clear, *we* were banging the screen door, not the mosquitoes, though they were nearly large enough to do so.)

Waiting for us would be the little black-and-white TV turned on to the Minnesota Twins baseball game, a jigsaw puzzle on the card table, and the smell of a ginormous bowl of buttered popcorn.

Yes, food was how Grandma, and I suppose many of the women of that generation, showed love. Enthusiastically consuming the food was how we recipients returned that love. For Grandma, a meal in which we took only a second helping of everything showed we clearly didn't love her. Our groans were ignored. "Oh, just have a little bit more. I don't want leftovers."

For a growing boy, time with Grandma was idyllic.

I know what you're thinking. That the glow of nostalgia has blinded me to my grandmother's shortcomings. Or that I've romanticized her and her fine-smelling kitchen to the point where she could hardly be a real, complex person.

Okay, in terms of shortcomings, I guess I did know my grandma to enjoy a juicy tidbit of gossip. She lived in a small town and liked to know everything going on.

As for her personal history, I know very little about Grandma's early life. It was only long after she was gone that I learned she had overcome significant adversity. When she was a little girl, her father was murdered. Then her husband, my grandpa, was verbally abusive the first dozen years of their marriage, until he stopped drinking.

To us children, Grandma projected the impression that she'd never had a bad day in her life.

In addition to those three boys just a little older than I, Grandma's twenty-one grandchildren also included little boys as well as girls of every age. And babies! There were always babies. Oh, Grandma loved to rock the babies and nibble their tiny toes.

For us older kids, she was always eager to hear what we were doing in school. My brother Cal was the eldest grandchild and a straight-A student. ("Thanks a lot, Cal" was our unanimous thought at his setting the bar so high.) Gary knew everything about cars. Barb played drums in the marching band. Cousin Tom and my sister Mary were artists. Bob was a star pitcher. Nancy was tall and slender, and her teacher suggested she could be a model. Cousin David and my little brother John were both so bright they could talk their way out of any trouble, and they got lots of practice. Terry had freckles and glowing golden-red hair and the accompanying gift of blarney. Vicky loved horses . . .

So many grandchildren! But, as I mentioned, I was Grandma's favorite.

Okay, she never put it in so many words, but it was clear to me. How she would light up when I came into view and envelop me in a soft, sweet-smelling hug. How she would make my favorite foods when she knew I was coming. How she exulted over any and all my achievements—in music or athletics or academics. (And they weren't all that tremendous.) How she was absolutely devastated when she learned I planned to go to seminary in California. "*Two thousand miles away!*" she lamented incredulously.

Oh, she loved me!

Imagine my surprise when I eventually discovered that every single one of my cousins and siblings also believed she or he was Grandma's favorite.

What?

Obviously, they were mistaken.

But of course, they weren't. Grandma treated each one of us as if he or she were the most cherished grandchild. She gushed over every one of us and made everyone's favorite dishes. She might have found some of us easier to like than others, though she never let on if that were so. I'm absolutely sure she *loved* each of us the same.

Loved us absolutely. Enormously. Without reserve or qualification. And with enough to go around for everybody. If you are not as lucky as I was in the grandmother department, I invite you to borrow mine to use as an example of this kind of unconditional love.

Grandma loved us beyond words. Though I never needed to give it any thought, I knew with every cell of my being that there was nothing I could do to change that love.

I could be an ax murderer and she wouldn't stop loving me. I could disappoint her, and sometimes I did. But nothing I could do would stop her from loving me. So I tried not to disappoint her, not in order to *earn* her love but in response to it.

Remember all that roughhousing my cousins did that so distressed Grandma and me? In hindsight, by inspecting that memory and looking closely at the look on Grandma's face and remembering the tone of her voice, I now realize I was the only one who was really that distressed. I think Grandma knew she made the roughhousing even more enjoyable for the boys if she pretended to be furious. The rumpus was always over in a few minutes, and I don't recall any lasting injuries to humans or furniture. She liked kids to be kids and to have some fun.

A grandmother's love—I like to think this is how God feels about each one of us. How God feels about you.

In the Church, we call it *grace*.

LIFE LESSONS

from

OUR ELDERS

INTRODUCTION TO CHAPLAINCY

After a quarter century in parish ministry, I needed a break from the hours and stress, so I had taken a position as a chaplain in a care center. Now all my parishioners were between 82 and 102 years of age. This was an interesting—and educational—experience.

First were the hearing challenges of my new flock. Twice in the first week, as I bent down to shake hands with a resident and introduce myself as "Chaplain Bill," I was greeted in reply with a broad smile and a hearty "Hullo, Captain Bill!"

I liked it, so I didn't correct them.

But I began to talk even louder and with exaggerated enunciation. On more than one occasion, back home in the evening, my kids would admonish me: "Dad, you're home. Stop shouting."

One of the perks of this midlife job shift was to once again be called "that fine young man," even though I was mere months away from my AARP card.

On the less happy side of things, it was eye-opening and disheartening to discover some of these nonagenarians were still as worried about their kids as I was about mine, especially since some of their "kids" were in their seventies! Mine were in elementary and middle school at the time, and I hadn't even come to the hard part yet (referring to teens and twenties, not seventies). Not only that, but those residents were often significantly anxious about their grandchildren and their great-grandchildren. I quickly realized that when you have two or three dozen family members, you have a lot of potential for heartache and anxiety.

Sigh.

ON BEING SANTA

Near the end of the staff meeting, my new boss turned to me and asked, "Will you play Santa for the employee Christmas party?"

Santa? The old, chubby guy?

This wasn't a request that made one feel like a jolly elf.

I was dumbfounded. For the first forty years of my life, I had been so slender that one of my "friends" described me as "prisoner-of-war scrawny." My supercharged metabolism roared like a Hong Kong Hula-Hoop factory in 1958. While training for a marathon in my early thirties, it was all I could do to keep 132 pounds on my six-foot frame. However, past forty that metabolism had slowed to a crawl, maybe a limp. Thus, having just turned fifty I had indeed begun to experience "middle" age.

Still . . . Santa Claus?

I was the new chaplain at a care center. Care centers don't employ a lot of men. It was evidently my turn to play Santa. Besides the whole girth issue, I wasn't a big fan of Santa Claus in general. Certainly I was at one time in my life, but now, as an adult—and particularly as a pastor—the whole idea of Santa made me uncomfortable. "Making a list, checking it twice," and rewarding kids for being good was blatantly antithetical to the Christian concept of grace, God's love for us regardless of our behavior. In addition, Santa seemed to me the very embodiment of the intense, crass commercialization of Christmas.

A pastor playing Santa Claus . . . Sigh.

But as the new guy, I was reluctant to refuse my boss's request. I forced a cheery smile and said I would do my best. The party was two weeks away and there would be dozens of little kids there, children of the staff.

Thus, a few days before Christmas, I found myself donning the costume—a rich red velvet suit, luxurious hair and beard, big black boots. And pillow. At least they felt I needed that.

I clomped into the party room crowded with employees and their kids. My jolly "Ho! Ho! Ho!" was met with squeals of delight—not only from the children but from the grown-ups as well. "Santa! Hi, Santa Claus!" Kids ran up and enveloped me in a giant group hug, their faces bright with excitement. They clung to my legs, stroked the velvet suit, and gently touched my splendid beard. After I was able to break free, I handed out candy canes and received more grateful hugs and high fives.

The kids were having *so* much fun that the Scrooge inside the Santa suit couldn't help himself. He was enjoying this gig. I made sure I interacted with each of the children—and each of the adults—at the party.

Then I figured that as long as I was all dressed up and sweating like a tuxedoed groom at an outdoor August wedding—this suit was truly made for the North Pole—I might as well spread some cheer among the residents as well. I wasn't sure what sort of reception to expect.

I walked next door to our short-term care unit and into the dining room. Two patients were seated at the round table nearest the door: a woman of about eighty and, opposite her, a man of the same vintage. They were eating without conversing; it was obvious they didn't know each other.

I strode over to the woman with a jolly "Merry Christmas!" and a "Ho! Ho! Ho!" Placing my white-gloved hand on her shoulder, I peered over the round spectacles perched on my nose and heartily inquired, "Have you been a good little girl this year?"

An impish grin crossed her face. Emphatically she shook her head. "No, I certainly have not!"

The man opposite was watching the two of us; at her remark, his eyebrows shot skyward. He made a beckoning gesture with his hand.

"Then send her over to my house!" he exclaimed.

My round little belly truly shook like a bowl full of jelly as I laughed and laughed, choosing not to reveal that underneath the fake beard and red suit and racy-sounding questions was the *chaplain.*

Next I visited patients in their rooms at the care center. Most were folks newly released from the hospital, recovering from hip and knee surgeries, plus a couple "MVAs"—motor vehicle accident victims. And a few folks with terminal cancer. All the residents had been through major transitions lately and were now facing the prospect of being away from home and family at Christmastime.

Picture it: A light, unexpected knock, and into their rooms stepped . . . Santa Claus. The response was universal: dropped jaws, sharp intakes of breath, eyes wide with delight. "Santa!" they exclaimed, reaching out to shake my hand, give a hug, stroke my beard. "Merry Christmas to *you*," they said. "Thanks so much for stopping by!"

Of course, unlike the children, these folks didn't "believe" in Santa Claus. Yet they obviously felt more kindly toward him than I had. For them, Santa represented hope, love, childlike trust, and wonderful memories. They were enchanted by a personal visit.

By this time, my frosty attitude had completely melted away in the warmth of their reactions. I felt so genuinely honored to play this revered figure, and soon I felt a profound sense of my own unworthiness to do so. Santa on a TV screen—telling kids they should ask for some plastic junk or, for the adult consumers, equating love with buying pricey diamonds for your wife—was one thing. But *being* Santa—knowing I was just a cranky, sweaty guy inside this velvet suit, a suit that was not just something for me to complain about having to put on, but a powerful symbol of magic and mystery and the spirit of giving—that was something else.

Christmas is the celebration of love in the flesh, I thought. Perhaps we should take it wherever we can find it.

And *be* it, wherever and however we can.

ON MINISTRY IN MEMORY CARE

Hands down, my favorite part of care center ministry was the residents in memory care. In my experience, the vast majority of memory-care residents are quite satisfied with their lives. While the situation is extremely painful for family members, the residents themselves, once they are far enough along to be in memory care, are content. Though they may not remember their children's names—or their own—they enjoy the meals (and especially the snacks) they are served. They like working on jigsaw puzzles, filling the bird feeders and then observing the brightly colored songbirds, doing art projects. Certainly the attention from the young women leading activities, and the tenderness of the aides as they brush the residents' hair and tuck them into bed, is greatly appreciated. The residents know they are safe . . . and they are loved.

On Tuesday afternoons I led a brief chapel service in memory care, always utilizing familiar biblical stories and favorite hymns. They never tired of "Amazing Grace" and "What a Friend We Have in Jesus." Neither did I, fortunately.

Then on Thursday afternoons I performed comedy with my ventriloquist's puppet, "Gramps." I was introduced to ventriloquism early in my career at a youth conference and have used a variety of puppets—birds, animals, and Gramps—in children's sermons over the years.

Little-known fact: there is no such thing as "throwing one's voice." The key to successful ventriloquism is (a) to get the audience's attention focused on the dummy, not the human, and (b) to avoid words with the letters *b* and *p*, which are difficult to enunciate without moving one's lips.

Gramps is a soft puppet, not a hard-body like Jeff Dunham's and other ventriloquists' dummies. Gramps is about twenty inches tall, has a mostly bald pate with a fringe of white hair, wears rimless spectacles, and is clothed in blue coveralls over a blue-and-white plaid shirt. In short—pun intended—he is adorable. And he is very witty, if I say so myself. Sometimes even I am surprised at what comes out of his mouth.

I purchased him when I was twenty-seven years old and it made perfect sense to name him *Gramps*. Today we share a remarkable resemblance, and soon I should perhaps start calling him *Son*.

Years ago I did stand-up for a time, but in the memory care unit I didn't have to come up with my own fresh material each week. So, this being Minnesota, we did a lot of Ole and Lena jokes and other classic groaners.

> Gramps: You know how when you see a flock of geese flying overhead, dey always fly in a V?
> Bill: Yeah.
> Gramps: And you no doubt have noticed that da one side of da V is usually longer than da other.
> Bill: Right . . .
> Gramps: Vy is dat?
> Bill: Umm, I don't know.
> Gramps: Has more geese in it!

Continuing the waterfowl theme—

Gramps: Which side of a duck has da most feathers?

Bill: Uhh . . . I give up.

Gramps: Da outside!

The residents chortled. "The outside!" they would repeat.

You get the idea. Corny jokes and memory loss go together like potatoes and gravy. Gramps and I were a hit. So much so that one Tuesday when I was leading the worship service (remember, worship on Tuesday, comedy on Thursday), one of the residents—in the middle of my sermon—called out loudly, "Where's Gramps?"

Being bored with a sermon reminds me of a story. Of course.

The chaplain leading the worship service at a care center had evidently gone on a bit long with his message, so one of the residents sitting in the back leaned over to her neighbor and declared loudly, "I'm so bored my butt fell asleep."

"I know," replied the woman next to her. "I heard it snore three times."

When people in the prison of late-stage memory loss are no longer able to recognize their family members or even say their own name, they are often still able to retrieve memories related to their faith life. Many times while attempting to talk with residents, I've wondered if the person even knew that anyone else was in the room with them. They would be slumped over in their wheelchairs, hands folded quietly in their laps, eyes shut or staring at nothing, like cats. But when I began to recite the Lord's Prayer or the Twenty-Third Psalm, the person would join right in, their voice growing louder and clearer with each line. This happened over and over.

It was the same with familiar music. People who no longer spoke would sing along with the old standards of their early years. Noted neurologist Oliver Sacks once said, "The past which is not recoverable in any other way is embedded, as if in amber, in the music . . ."

One of our residents, whom I had known for several years, eventually suffered a massive stroke. All the color had left her face, she had largely lost her ability to speak, and she lay in her bed for days, staring at the window. Knowing she had served for decades as a church choir director, I brought a hymnal with me when I went into her room for a visit one afternoon, and I sat down next to her bed and began to sing hymns to her. Rather, I sang them "with" her, as she immediately joined me in singing, her eyes bright. She sang flawlessly, for nearly an hour, and she knew the words to every hymn.

She died the next day.

Singing comes from a different part of the brain than regular speech. I had a seminary classmate who had the most severe stutter I had ever encountered. However, when he sang he had no speech impediment whatsoever and his beautiful tenor voice rang clearly through the chapel. The same thing when he prayed aloud: no stutter. Fascinating!

Unlike speech, singing and praying come from the right hemisphere of the brain. In fact, there is a choir, Stroke-a-Chord, outside Melbourne, Australia, composed of stroke survivors with aphasia, which means they have largely lost the ability to speak. Yet they can sing!

What an amazing gift. Now that I am back in the pastorate, I like to bring along our hymnal when I visit our parishioners in memory care. Together we make a joyful noise unto the Lord.

For the person with memory loss, music therapy provides a number of benefits. Hearing a familiar song can allow them to tap into memories associated with the song or that time in their life. Listening to familiar music and singing along, perhaps clapping, can give someone with dementia a sense of accomplishment and control and naturally serves as a mood brightener. It can even help relieve pain.

DEATHBED VIGIL

I concentrated on not allowing my left eyebrow to rise, as it usually does when I am feeling skeptical. As the new chaplain conducting the memorial service, I put on my thoughtful face instead.

The sixty-five-year-old son of the deceased was telling about how the six resident cats of our long-term care facility had gathered in his mother's room for a deathbed vigil during the final two days of her life. The son was comforted by the cats and found their company profoundly meaningful, even miraculous. I thought it was a nice coincidence and maybe not even that: the cats had free run of the floor, and the son, from the way he was talking about them, was obviously a cat lover. Probably word had spread through the cat community that free tummy rubs were available in room 314.

A week or so later, another resident, eighty-eight-year-old Monica, took a turn for the worse. She was now clearly in the "actively dying" process. Monica had always enjoyed the cats, but never had more than one or two been in her room at the same time. Now I watched as Tulip, the orange tabby and our friendliest feline, hopped up on the bed and snuggled in next to Monica's arm, while the other five took up posts around the room. As the hours eased by, the other cats occasionally slipped out briefly to eat, drink, or stretch their legs, but not Tulip. According to the family, for the final forty-eight hours of their mom's life, Tulip never once left her side.

Over the following months, I observed the phenomenon several more times. Not with every dying resident, but at least a third of the time the cats gathered around to participate in a resident's transition to the next life. One time, a resident's son who was keeping vigil for his mother noted the two cats in the windowsill at the foot of the bed and commented to me, "Huh. I never saw a cat in my mom's room before."

By then a believer, I reported matter-of-factly, but gently, "They're here because your mom is dying."

Noting *his* raised eyebrow, I added kindly, "We see it frequently. Would you like me to take the cats out?"

"No, no." He smiled. "That's really something. I like that the cats are here."

After talking with the long-term staff, I discovered no one had ever observed more than two cats in a resident's room at the same time *except* when the resident was nearing death. If I had ever looked up from my work to see all six of them meowing at my office door, I would have been pretty nervous.

When I went to serve as chaplain at another facility, I soon discovered that one of their two resident cats was also a proficient death predictor. Actually, *proficient* understates her performance. She was virtually foolproof. I cannot remember one time in the four years I served there that the cat was not present for a resident's death. In fact, one day a dying woman was discharged from the hospital and moved into our care center to spend her last few days. The facility had three wings and sixty-four residents, but within one hour the cat had found and snuggled up to our new resident, and she stayed there until the end.

How do the cats know someone is dying? Stories about animals acting in this way with owners they have lived with for ten or fifteen years make more sense; pets grow attuned to their owners after long, daily association. But our facilities had dozens of residents, and each cat had minimal contact with any one of them.

And why do they gather around to hold vigil with the person leaving this world?

My friend suggested maybe they were just seeking out warmth. And it is true that in the late stages of illness, a person's thermostat often gets out of whack and they get quite warm. We often put cool, damp washcloths on the foreheads of dying people. But for a cat not to leave the person's side for forty-eight hours—not to eat, drink, or use the litter box once in two days?

Some scientists believe the cats might be picking up on a "death smell," certain chemicals that are released just before death.

Cats do have a keen sense of smell. They have also been known to "sniff out" illness. A nurse I knew told me that one evening as she was lying in bed reading, her cat jumped up on the bed and started pawing at her chest. She shooed the cat away. But over the next several days, her pet kept it up. One night the woman woke to the cat actually biting her in the breast. She vaguely recalled hearing a story of a cat detecting cancer, so she decided to get it checked out. And indeed, she had breast cancer.

Holding vigil? Detecting cancer?

Got me. Let's just call it a holy mystery.

GHOSTS IN THE CARE CENTER?

To follow up on cats in the care center: This happened in the first care center I served, about a dozen years ago. Most afternoons Evelyn stood in the doorway of her private room next to the nursing station, invariably dressed in her diaphanous white nightgown and matching terry-cloth slippers. With her short, white hair and stick-thin figure, she might have, from a distance— well, quite a distance—been mistaken for a pre-adolescent. Evelyn was eighty-six and fully capable mentally. I sometimes stopped by and worked with her on her daily crossword puzzle for a few minutes. I was of little help, as she was much more skilled than I. Had she possessed any close relatives, she might well have lived somewhere other than our facility, where she had been for five years.

For hours each day she stood guard in the doorway of her single room, looking up and down the hallway, eager to see what was going on. She made no secret of her interest in the private conversations of the nursing staff as they discussed their weekend plans and personal affairs. As one of our nurses said, "We are her entertainment."

Evelyn appeared to be fragile. Actually, she was a tiger. As she grew frailer, she began to regularly punch her white call light to summon a nurse, then demand to have her oxygen turned up. If the staff refused her requests, she would do it herself, to levels far above doctors' orders.

Eventually Evelyn suffered a number of falls, and ultimately she broke her pelvis, which landed her in the hospital. Two days later Evelyn was, of course, still hospitalized.

And now—back to the cats!

At about three thirty that afternoon back at the care center, Sheba, one of our resident felines, was sleeping soundly on the ledge of the nurses' desk—a few feet from Evelyn's vacant room. The nurse in charge of that wing was doing paperwork at the desk when suddenly Sheba raised her head, her ears perked. Then the cat scrambled to her feet, faced Evelyn's doorway, flattened her ears, arched her back, and hissed.

The nurse turned in the direction Sheba was facing in order to see what was causing her reaction. There was no one there. Nothing out of the ordinary. The nurse puzzled over this.

Then the white call light over Evelyn's door turned on!

The nurse stared at the light and blinked a couple of times as she reminded herself that Evelyn was in the hospital. And that Evelyn did not have a roommate. More than a bit unnerved, the nurse slowly rose and peered into Evelyn's room. Empty. She tiptoed her way to the bathroom door and tentatively peeked around it. No one, no one at all.

She walked to the bed and pushed the button to turn the call light off. She turned it on and off a few times. It worked perfectly.

A bit later, the hospital called to say Evelyn had died at one o'clock that afternoon . . .

Personally, I think the call light was Evelyn saying, "I *told* you I needed more oxygen!"

The next day at lunchtime, I relayed this story to four or five of my work colleagues gathered around a table in the cafeteria. As I concluded, the only other male at the table, a rec therapist named Jerry, moaned, "Ohhhh. Don't tell me things like that. That creeps me out!" He shuddered. "I'll have to sleep with the light on all week."

Another colleague said, "Wait till you hear this one! True story." With a look of terror on his face, Jerry gathered his things and fled. We chuckled. She continued: "I used to work at the care center down the street. There was a long-term resident who every night around one o'clock needed to go to the bathroom. He would turn on his call light, and an aide would help him get out of bed and get to the toilet. Well, this went on night after night for two or three years. Finally, he passed away. The next night . . ." She paused for dramatic effect, head cocked slightly, eyes wide, looking at each of us in turn. We stared back at her, rapt. The hair on my arms stood on end.

She took a breath and then continued, "The next night at one o'clock . . . the call light over the door . . . to his now-empty room . . . turned on. No one there. In fact, at one o'clock each night, for the next two weeks the call light turned on."

ON DEATH

Though I had officiated at dozens of funerals in my years as a parish pastor, serving as the chaplain in a care center brought me into daily contact with people in the dying process. We averaged nine deaths per month. Among the many lessons I learned is chronically ill people have an astonishing amount of control over *when* they die.

An eighty-seven-year-old man came into our transitional care unit following a major stroke. He was somewhat conscious and able to speak a bit, but he had suffered significant damage and was not expected to live more than a day or two. Prior to the stroke, he had been vibrant and strong, six-foot-two with a full head of salt-and-pepper hair. A widower, he had a large family, and his room immediately filled with children and grandchildren. They brought flowers and played his favorite music on a CD player. After the initial shock of the situation faded, his room frequently rang with laughter as the family recounted favorite family stories.

He did not die. Day after day. Almost two weeks went by, and the medical staff was astounded he was still around. One Friday afternoon I thought I would pay a quick visit before I left for the weekend. In his room on the second floor, I found a visitor I had not previously met. It was a son who had been in Greece and had just now finally been able to return to see his father.

"Ah," I thought to myself, "now George can die. I'll bet he is gone when I return on Monday."

He died that night.

We had another resident in our long-term care unit, Grace, a tiny woman with gray hair pinned neatly in a bun. During the day, she was liberated by her wheelchair. (The phrase *confined to a wheelchair* has the reality of the situation backward.) She received a visit every day from her granddaughter and the granddaughter's three well-behaved preschool children. (The granddaughter also had *six* older children in school. They came each weekend.) The great-grandma literally lived for these daily visits, as the kids clambered up onto her lap in the wheelchair, with their wet kisses and hugs, and presented her with their lovingly made art projects, which the granddaughter then posted around the room.

The granddaughter, also a tiny woman, was visibly pregnant with child number ten when her grandma took a turn for the worse and the doctors gave Grace a week to live, two at the most.

But that baby wasn't due for six more weeks.

We on the staff knew this great-grandma wasn't going anywhere until she got to hold that baby. Day after day, week after week, Grace defied the medical odds. Finally, one day the granddaughter arrived with the usual three preschoolers in tow . . . plus a bundle in her arms. Great-grandma held this baby and blessed it, like Simeon and Anna in the Temple with the baby Jesus (Luke 2:21–38), and then, that evening, Grace left in peace.

Over the course of my seven years as a chaplain, I had the deep and holy privilege of accompanying several hundred people on their dying journeys. I learned that the vast majority of people follow nearly identical stages toward death. Though I am not medically trained, I can now simply look at a dying person and usually predict, very closely, how much time they have remaining. Just as we know how a one-hour-old baby looks and acts, and how that changes as the baby grows to a week or a month old, care center employees can usually discern whether a person is one month, one week, or one day away from exiting this life.

With a few weeks to go, people often lose interest in the things that had been their very lifeblood previously, whether it's updates on a sports team or news of their grandchildren. They start to disengage from this life. When they are unable to get out of bed into their wheelchair, and start to talk and eat very little, they are likely within a couple weeks of death. But people can live an astonishingly long time with no food as long as they have water. When they show no interest in water, then we are within a few days. Finally, the person stops responding altogether and we are getting closer. There usually is a period of very regular breathing for a day or two. This is followed by irregular respiration, as much as a minute or more between breaths. In my experience, this stage usually lasts two to twelve hours.

This irregular breathing can be upsetting to the family members gathered at the person's bedside. But once they get accustomed to the intermittent respiration, those who are gathered usually return to sharing memories of their loved one:

"Remember the time Dad fell off the dock . . ."

"I'll never forget when the dog ate Grandma's soufflé . . ."

They laugh at the recollections. And then someone will look over at the figure on the bed and say, "How long has it been since her last breath?" And the person is gone.

That quietly.

Nothing dramatic about it.

Peaceful. Holy.

But fairly often, people will refuse to die as long as someone is in the room with them. This is especially true for folks who never wanted to have a fuss made over them. They prefer to slip away alone; though, personally, I don't believe anyone dies completely alone (Luke 16:22).

One time, a large family kept vigil for a month straight. All day and all night, no exceptions, someone was with their loved one. They read letters to their mom, spoke of childhood memories, or simply sat in a pleasant silence. Then some new folks—distant relatives—came into town. They all decided to slip out for a quick breakfast. Mom took the opportunity to slip out herself. I kind of think if they hadn't left, she'd *still* be there.

We also often find it's helpful for the family to give the person permission to go, to reassure the dying loved one that those left behind will be okay.

Occasionally in the last day or so of life, people will begin talking to loved ones who have gone on before. I especially recall this one lovely man whose wife had preceded him in death five years earlier. As he was slipping away, he looked over near the window and began talking in loving tones to the one whom only he could see.

A somewhat similar experience happened with Harriet. Harriet was a dignified ninety-year-old who spent her days in the social area of her unit in long-term care. She had thick, shoulder-length gray hair and always wore blue sweaters to match her eyes. You could tell she had been a physically strong woman at one time, but now her back condition made it more comfortable to lie down than to sit up, so when not in bed, she stretched out flat in a recumbent wheelchair. Harriet had gradually lost her eyesight, and when I met her, she was entirely blind. In fact, she no longer bothered to open her eyes at all. In the two years I knew her, I never saw her sit up or open her eyes.

But Harriet was extremely sharp, and I enjoyed visiting with her each day for a few minutes. We talked current events, weather, her childhood on a South Dakota farm. Her son Jim visited from his home thirty miles away every single day. (I've mentioned this a time or two to my own kids—planting the seed.) He was a large man, with a ruddy face and a white shock of hair, always pleasant as he chatted with the staff and so kind and gentle with his mom, holding her hand, sometimes stroking her hair.

Harriet had not changed much in the two years I had known her, but eventually her medical condition began to worsen. The nurse practitioner thought she was probably in her last couple of months. About two weeks after this assessment, Jim came for his daily visit. Afterward, he related a story:

"I wheeled Mom into the library, where we could be alone. We chatted a bit and then sat in a companionable silence. All of a sudden, Mom sat straight up! She opened her eyes. Wide. And, Chaplain Bill, her eyes never looked so blue. She stared straight ahead and got a huge smile on her face. Then she lay back down . . . and was gone."

After a holy silence, Jim continued, "It was such a privilege that I got to witness that. Clearly, she was seeing the next world."

And what a privilege it was for me to hear that account.

God bless you, Harriet.

On Funerals

I t has been my deep and holy privilege to officiate at hundreds of funerals.

Many laypeople are surprised to find out most clergy enjoy doing funerals. (That is, the funerals of old people, whose lives are complete. The funeral of a young person is an entirely different matter.) In fact, most of us pastors vastly prefer officiating at funerals to performing weddings. A funeral has fewer moving pieces. Literally. By that, I mean funerals have no batsh**-crazy Bridezillas to worry about, no controlling mothers of the bride trying to make up for their own disappointing nuptials, no drunken groomsmen. (In one church I served, the soundboard was inside the janitor's closet next to the sanctuary. Right before a wedding was to begin, our female associate pastor opened the door of the closet to turn on the mics—only to find a groomsman peeing into the sink.) You get my point.

The primary purposes of a Christian funeral are to give thanks, to comfort one another, and to say goodbye.

We say thanks to God for the gift of this person and for all the ways in which our lives have been enriched through knowing her. We gather as a community to support one another in our loss.

And we release our loved one back into God's embrace and thank God for the promise that love never ends.

I once heard a story, possibly factual, certainly true (in that it illuminates the human condition, whether it actually happened or not).

When we who are in charge of such things plan worship services, whether it's a typical Sunday service, a wedding, or a funeral, we want things to go a certain way. We do our very best to make sure things go exactly as planned. But they rarely do.

In this story, the deceased was a huge Elvis Presley fan. She had been to two of his concerts and owned all his records. So it was decided that as the family entered the worship space at the beginning of the service, "Love Me Tender" would be softly filling the sanctuary.

But when the day came and the family started down the aisle, the funeral director hit the wrong cut on the CD. Instead of "Love Me Tender," the gathered loved ones heard the jaunty horn lines of "Return to Sender."

Which is perfect! That is precisely what we are doing at a funeral. Our loved ones do not belong to us. We merely borrow them for a while. And eventually we have to return them to the One who loves them even more than we do—the One who fashioned them and, for a time, loaned them to us.

A funeral is also sometimes used as a teaching tool. It is common for fundamentalist pastors to use a funeral as an opportunity to literally try to scare the hell out of people. "You, too, will lie in a casket someday. Repeat the Four Spiritual Laws or spend eternity on a rotisserie." That sort of thing.

However, I once attended a memorable funeral that was used as a positive and very moving teaching opportunity. My cousin Terry, four years older than I, was a remarkable person, freckle-faced and red-haired, with a winning smile and the Irishman's gift of gab. While growing up, I very much envied his easygoing confidence in any social situation. Terry became a very successful sales manager and married a lovely college classmate named Joanne. Together, they had two beautiful children.

At age forty-four, Terry died of cancer. I was devastated.

I wasn't alone. Terry's family was active in a large suburban, upper-middle-class Catholic church, and over a thousand people gathered there for his funeral. I sat in the back, wishing to remain anonymous, barely able to control my emotions. The very gifted and compassionate priest led a warm and meaningful service, though through the haze of my grief I was only half-aware of the proceedings. I was looking down at my feet when the words of the priest slowly formed into meaning in my brain: "Now Joanne would like to say a few words."

What? I panicked. I was already just barely holding it together. Now, I believe it's perfectly fine to cry at a funeral. But I was afraid I wasn't going to just shed a few tears. My grief was so intense I thought I might start sobbing and wailing, maybe even throw up. I desperately wanted to flee. But I was in the middle of a pew, a dozen people on either side of me. Trapped.

I watched with trepidation as Joanne made her way to the pulpit, a green backpack slung over one shoulder. She thanked everyone for coming and for loving Terry and the family. She mentioned all the support the family had received during his illness.

Then she said words to this effect: "This illness has been terrible, of course. But at the same time, cancer has taught us a lot of things. And I would like to share with you some of the things we have learned in these past few months. Terry, as you know, always dreamed of being a successful businessman." She pulled the backpack off her shoulder and set it on the pulpit. Then she reached in and pulled out a copy of *Forbes* magazine and showed the cover to the crowd. "Well, Terry achieved that goal. But cancer taught us that success in business doesn't matter." And Joanne tossed the magazine over her shoulder onto the ground.

"We have a nice house. Four bedrooms. Large lot. Terry was so proud of our house, and he always wanted everything to look just right." Joanne reached into the backpack again and pulled out a *House Beautiful* magazine. She held it aloft. "Cancer taught us that houses don't matter," she said and tossed the magazine over her other shoulder.

She paused to look around at all of those freshly scrubbed, beautifully coiffed forty-somethings gathered in the church before going on. "As you know, Terry *always* liked to look good . . . and he did." Smiles and a few chuckles from the crowd. In my experience, he was always impeccably dressed. I wondered if he did yardwork in his dress clothes. Joanne continued, "In recent weeks he said to his friends, 'You'll be able to recognize me in heaven. I'll be the only one wearing a necktie.'"

Even I had relaxed to the point that I could join in the laughter on that one. Joanne peered into the backpack again and pulled out a *GQ* magazine. The model on the front didn't look any handsomer than Terry always had.

Joanne held up the *GQ* and said, "In the last few months, Terry didn't look so good. But we found that it didn't matter." She flipped the *GQ* into the air, and it splayed onto the floor.

"For years Terry's dream was to someday own a Porsche. Four years ago he achieved that dream," she said then, and by now we could predict the fate of the copy of *Car and Driver* she pulled out, a beautiful black Porsche convertible on the cover. "He *loved* that car. He kept it spotless. He washed and vacuumed it every Saturday. He shined the tires! But this year we learned . . . cars don't matter."

Joanne looked at the magazines strewn around her, then out at her friends. I looked back at her, now extremely grateful I hadn't found a way to escape the sanctuary before I got to hear her speak.

"Cancer taught us that *all* that matters is your relationship with God and with the people in your life," she said.

On War

Istarted my time as a chaplain in early 2002, shortly after the
9/11 tragedy.

As a parish pastor yet for a few months beyond the at-
tacks, I weighed in from the pulpit on the biblical/theological aspects of the growing drumbeat toward war and the invasion of
Iraq. We had the world's sympathy. But it seemed to me this was
an opportune time to show the rest of the globe how we could find
new ways of responding to violence, especially since the attackers
weren't Iraqis.

However, as a chaplain, and especially a new chaplain, I chose
to remain silent for a number of reasons. First, these folks were a
captive audience. Unlike parishioners, they couldn't up and find
a new church if the pastor ticked them off. Second, I mistakenly
thought they probably weren't paying that much attention to current events. So I kept my homilies rather generic—peace, comfort,
hope, that sort of thing.

But I was wrong. People wanted to discuss the invasion talk.
They would bring it up. All our residents had lived through World
War II; many of them had served. One woman showed off the

medal and accompanying article about her brother, who, while serving in the infantry, had leaped on top of a live grenade to save his compatriots, sacrificing himself. She was so proud of her little brother, who died at just nineteen, and still so sad almost sixty years later. Of course.

Another woman proudly showed off photos from her service as a Women's Army Corps nurse. Thinking back now, it seemed the men were more reticent about the particulars of their service.

One of our residents was a Polish immigrant. It hadn't occurred to me that he always wore long-sleeved shirts until one day, as he reached for his coffee, his sleeve slid up from his wrist a ways and I saw the angry blue numbers tattooed across his forearm. I had never seen such a thing in person, but my heart went cold as I instantly realized what it was: a memento from the Auschwitz concentration camp.

Having been born seven years after the victorious conclusion of World War II, it somehow had never occurred to me that we might have lost the war. Pretty much all I picked up in my childhood was that World War II was the most glorious time in our country's history. We were 100 percent the good guys, and we had saved the world for democracy. The war was the springboard for the prosperity and world leadership the US now enjoyed.

There was none of the moral ambiguity of Korea or, especially, of Vietnam.

Now, hearing our residents' stories of their daily fear and anxiety through World War II, I gained a new appreciation for what each person had gone through. Writing a daily letter to their sweetheart somewhere in the Pacific and waiting anxiously to receive a blessedly big batch at a time in return. Observing the Gold Stars in the windows of neighbors and friends and dreading the potential arrival of the military messenger appearing at their own door with tragic news.

All this talk of war in early 2002 was triggering anew these old memories. And not one of the residents who shared an opinion was in favor of a military response to 9/11. Not one! "Don't they know that war doesn't solve anything? Oh, Chaplain Bill, I hope they don't start bombing and sending in troops! I pray every day for a peaceful response."

Those who have been in war know we need to find a new way.

ON OLD AGE

I like to come to church. (Fortunately!)

When all week long in wider society I have been bombarded with lies, I like to come to church to hear the truth. Jesus said, "You shall know the truth, and the truth shall set you free." So true!

Society tells us a list of lies: a new car is necessary for happiness; violence is a legitimate and effective way to solve problems; going to bed on the first date is a good idea; fidelity in relationships is optional; professional athletes, judging by their salaries, are one hundred times more valuable than schoolteachers.

As a pastor, I like to do my best to halt the spread of another pervasive lie: being old is bad.

"Gray hair is a crown of glory," says Proverbs 16:31. "It is gained in a righteous life." Most countries and cultures know this; only in the Western world have we fallen so far from the biblical model. In the US, youth is worshipped and old age is at best a joke and at worst a horror. You're supposed to be embarrassed if you've made the unfortunate mistake of growing old.

My brother-in-law Mark has been a medical missionary in Tanzania for over thirty years. He has noted that as his hair and beard turned gray, he got more respect in that country. In fact, he has been made an honorary Maasai elder. Mark and his wife, Linda, come back to the States every other summer to vacation and itinerate, to visit the churches that support their work. When he returns home to Tanzania, the people there greet him with big smiles and open arms and say to him, "Welcome back, Dr. Jacobson. You look well: older and fatter."

Older and fatter. Ah, to live in Tanzania!

I have always loved older folks, even before I became one. I grew up around a lot of old folks, and it always seemed to me they were funnier, wiser, more resilient, and even more spontaneous and open to new experiences than many of the younger folks around them.

When I was a kid, my aunts and uncles on my dad's side were already in their sixties and seventies. My grandfather was ninety-nine years old when I was born. He had been born in 1853. It is always a conversation piece to be able to say that someone who knew me could remember when Abraham Lincoln was president.

One day when my grandpa Heck (full name *Hector*) was a hundred years old and still living in his house, he was sitting on the porch when a neighbor walked by and inquired how he was. "Just fine," he replied. "Well—except for my left knee. It's pretty sore and, for the life of me, I can't figure out what's wrong with it."

"Well," the neighbor responded gently, "you don't suppose it could just be old age?"

"No, can't be," my grandpa said. "The other knee's the same age, and it don't hurt a bit."

That same year while out walking, Grandpa Heck was run over by a truck. Despite two broken legs, he lived another year and a half. At the time of the incident, one of the locals wrote to his brother, who had moved out of state, "Old Mr. Chadwick got hit by a truck last week. Totaled the truck."

I once asked my dad if he had any theories as to why his father lived so long. "He never worried about a thing. He just took each day as it came." (I wish he were around now to give lessons on how to achieve that sort of equanimity.)

At any rate, my interesting aged relatives provided inspiration to the young folks around them to keep living life as long as it lasted.

My dad's sister Flossie married for the first time at age seventy.

My dad's brother Ernie was widowed twice and married for the third time at age eighty-five. Following the brief ceremony, he drove with his seventy-eight-year-old bride, Nettie, from Minneapolis to Michigan for their honeymoon. Ernie smoked cigarettes until he was eighty, when he switched to a pipe. He died at ninety-eight. Nettie lived to be a hundred and seven! She lived in three centuries, from 1895 to 2002.

My great-grandfather died at age eighty-six after being gored by a bull. As the story goes, he went for a walk on a Sunday morning and on his way home decided to take the shortcut through the pasture.

Moral of the story #1: *Beware of shortcuts in life.*

Moral of the story #2: *Don't skip church.*

(And then on the other hand, there's my maternal great-grandfather, who at age thirty-six was murdered in an arson fire.)

I hope to have an interesting death too.

Though not for a while.

When my father turned sixty, he had a child in college, a child in junior high, a child in elementary school, and one in *kindergarten*! Even when he was eighty, whenever people would ask my dad how many children he had, he would answer, "Four . . . so far."

Which reminds me of a story. (Everything does now, at my age.)

An old gentleman's longtime physician finally retired, so the man had to find a new doctor for his annual physical. The young doctor finished examining the eighty-year-old and remarked, "You are in excellent shape. You're good to go for years yet. I'm curious, how old was your father when he died?"

"Did I say my father was dead?"

"What! You're eighty years old and your father is still alive?"

"Yep. One hundred and four and going strong."

"Wow," replied the doctor. "Well, how old was your grandfather when he died?"

"Did I say my grandfather was dead?"

"Oh, come now! Don't try to tell me your grandfather is still alive."

"Still alive. One hundred and twenty-six. Not only that, he's getting married next week."

"One hundred and twenty-six years old! . . . But why would he want to get married at one hundred and twenty-six?"

"Did I say he *wanted* to get married?"

One of my parishioners, a hale and hearty and ridiculously healthy ninety-three-year-old, recently observed, "You know you are getting old when you take your wife and four kids out to dinner and *everyone* gets the senior discount."

To those in my congregation who are chronologically gifted, I try not to brag too much about the robust lives so often enjoyed by the elderly in my own family—because, of course, that's not always the case.

Some of my parishioners, because of failing health, are no longer able to serve in active ways. When I was a young associate pastor in my first congregation, I had the privilege to become friends with a very old parishioner named Mrs. McCormack. Mrs. McCormack had been exceedingly active in the church all her life. She was a deacon and involved with women's circles, and she had been the Sunday School superintendent for decades. You get the picture.

But when I met her, she was quite weak and confined to her bed. When I was visiting in her home one day, she said to me, "You know, Pastor Bill, I can't do like I used to do. But there is one thing I can still do. I can pray. I keep the church calendar next to my bed here. And any time anything is going on, I am praying. When you are teaching the Bethel Series teachers Monday evening, I am praying for you. When you are with the confirmation kids on Wednesday evening, I am praying for you. When the church council is meeting, when the Sunday worship service is going on . . ."

Wow! I contend no one in that congregation of six hundred members was serving more faithfully and powerfully than this frail, bedridden woman. People of faith, will you please follow the example of Mrs. McCormack?

I also tell my aged and infirm parishioners this: all your life you have been doing and giving, and feeling good about that. It feels good to give and to help. "It is more blessed to give than to receive," said Jesus.

I ask them now to gracefully allow others to help them. That's a gift—to be a gracious receiver (the *gracious* part is very important, as anyone who has ever taken care of a less-than-gracious person knows) and to let other people feel good in the act of helping them.

"Octogenarians, nonagenarians, centenarians," I say, "we need you. We learn from you. We honor you. We celebrate you. We thank you. We praise God for you!"

On Baldness

During one otherwise unnotable afternoon, my ninth-grade science teacher told our class baldness is inherited through the mother's side.

I immediately draped myself dramatically over my desk. (Did I mention my radical ninth-grade transformation into obnoxiousness?) I fake-cried. Well, it was *partially* fake.

In ninth grade, I had beautifully thick and wavy hair. In a few years, it would flow luxuriously down to my shoulders. With these enviable goods on my head, you can't blame me for assuming I took after my paternal grandfather, who had a full head of hair up until his death at 102.

But no. Apparently his hair wouldn't mean anything for me. And my *mom's* dad had been almost completely bald by the age of thirty. Both of his sons likewise. Indeed, even my mother's hair was much thinner than my father's, despite her being female and sixteen years younger!

A bleak future awaited me. I tried to console myself by remembering that at least I had a few good years ahead. I didn't have it as bad as a kid in my high school who had lost his hair due to illness years earlier. He recovered, but his hair never grew back. His "friends" called him *Brunswick* (for the bowling ball company).

In recent years, scientists have found that one's mother's X chromosome is not the *only* factor that contributes to baldness, but in my case it proved to be enough. By the time I finished seminary at age twenty-four, it looked as if my science teacher had been right. Sigh.

I don't quite understand why, when it's no longer okay for kind and respectable people to make fun of those who are [insert almost any human condition here], it's still okay to make fun of bald men. Obviously those making bald jokes have never read 2 Kings. Some boys made fun of the prophet Elijah: "Get out of here, baldy!" He called down a curse upon the boys, and two bears roared out of the woods to maul forty-two of them. (Okay, not one of the prophet's shining moments . . . but I bet no one made a bald joke in Elijah's presence for a good long while, either.)

I've heard all the jokes a thousand times.

"God only made so many perfect heads. The rest God covered in hair."

"Men who are bald in back are lovers. Men who are bald in front are thinkers. Men who are bald in both front and back only think they are lovers."

"What do you call a louse on a bald man's head? Homeless."

And then there are the answers:

"I'm so handsome, my face just keeps getting longer!"

"I'm not bald. This is a solar collector for a sex machine."

Here's my own favorite rejoinder. I've heard the follically challenged Baptist preacher Tony Campolo tell this excellent zinger a number of times:

"The way I look at it is like this," he says. "At birth we are all given the same amount of hormones. If some of you guys want to use yours for growing hair, that's your business."

A few years back, when I was the chaplain in a care center, it was my practice to make daily rounds, going to each nurse's station to see if there were anyone with special needs that day whom I might visit. One morning a nurse responded, "Nothing going on today." Then a thought occurred to her: "I *am* getting my hair cut tonight with a new stylist. Maybe you could pray for my hair." (She had gorgeous, long blond hair.)

I cocked my head and said to her, "Really?" I pointed to my bald pate. "If I were any good at praying for hair, would I look like this?" She stared at my head and, with a look of horror, waved her hands back and forth in a *no* gesture, exclaiming, "Good point! *Don't* pray for my hair!"

As mentioned, my maternal grandfather was mostly bald his entire adult life. He just had a circular fringe of hair around the sides. One blustery, snowy day when he was in his seventies, he bundled up and walked the two blocks up the street to the barbershop. He quickly closed the door behind him, brushed the snow off his shoulders, stomped his feet, and said to his longtime barber, "Wally, do you mind if I leave my boots on?"

Wally looked him up and down, then stated drily, "I don't mind if you leave your *hat* on."

HOLY FOOLS

H*oly Fools*, we called ourselves. Knowing we were at least half right.

Our group was made up of a gaggle of junior- and senior-high kids from our church; an adult advisor or two; and I, the associate pastor. Once a month, we donned clown makeup and costumes and visited local children's hospitals and homes for the elderly. (This was before Stephen King made clowns scary.)

An ancient Christian tradition uses the clown as a symbol for Jesus, for he was the One who shattered all expectations concerning propriety and power. Jesus was "God's fool." The symbol fell out of favor for a few centuries. During that time, the Church concentrated on being dull, dour, and dreary, operating on the deep fear that somewhere someone might be enjoying herself.

But by the 1970s, things had loosened up a bit—in fact, more than a bit. Sanctuaries everywhere were stuffed to bursting with guitars and balloons in the church's frantic pursuit of "relevance." Following the lead of some creative folks, we formed a clowning troupe. With their parents' help, the teens made their own costumes, sewing outrageous creations and rummaging through their fathers' wardrobes for goofy ties and crazy shoes, which were not hard to find in the 1970s.

The kids designed their own clown faces, starting with a white background and adding designs in red, blue, or green. We learned that "clown law" requires that each clown face, anywhere it appears in the world, be unique. There's something powerful in that idea. It reflects our belief that God loves and cares for each individual on the planet—"numbers the hairs on our heads," as Jesus put it.

There's something magical about clown makeup, and not just for the audience. Kids who normally trembled if required to simply hand out Sunday bulletins at the sanctuary entrance could, when dressed in silly suits and big, red rubber noses, calmly talk and hold hands with patients three years old or a hundred and three. Adolescent anxieties about acne, popularity, and self-image were rendered temporarily impotent by the persona of a clown. As clowns, the kids didn't have to act "cool." They were unbound from their teenage insecurities and freed for service, a bit like the women and men whom Jesus made whole.

Sometimes our clown troupe led worship services in our own church, but mostly we climbed aboard Big Blue, the church bus, and made house calls. There's something about a whole bus full of clowns—including the driver! Big Blue never failed to elicit surprised smiles and eager waves everywhere we went. A simple cruise around the block was in itself a ministry to an often dreary world.

When we led worship, we did so in mime. But when we visited nursing homes or hospitals, we always talked with people—and, especially, *listened* to people. We didn't really have a lot else we could do. A few magic tricks. A couple of songs. But mostly we didn't attempt to put on a show. We practiced what is often called the "ministry of presence," simply being there with people who might not have a lot of attention being paid to them.

In the Gospels, Jesus performs some flashy miracles: driving demons into pigs, multiplying the loaves and fishes, giving sight to the blind. But some of the time, he simply hangs out. Luke gives us no details about the conversation Jesus had when he went to lunch at the tax collector Zacchaeus's house (Luke 19:1–10), but I'm guessing that when somebody was one-on-one with Jesus, Jesus wasn't primarily teaching; he was listening. As Lloyd John Ogilvie has noted, the subject of the conversation between Jesus and Zacchaeus was probably . . . Zacchaeus! And the tax collector came away transformed.

At any rate, we clowns simply tried to carry on this idea, incarnating a little bit of God's love and care in the flesh.

As one might expect, very ill children lying morosely in hospital beds suddenly squealed with delight when a clown peeked around the door. And the sparkle would return to the eyes of weary nursing home residents when in the presence of a dozen Holy Fools.

One Saturday morning, a dozen of us clowns traipsed into Maple Manor Health Care Center. We did our usual two-minute group "show" at the beginning, then split up and began visiting with the elderly residents. I was in my red-and-white-striped, puffy-sleeved costume; purple patent leather shoes; cardinal-red wig; and makeup. I pulled up a chair at a round table where two elderly men were seated, having their midmorning coffee.

I turned to the man on my left. He had a full head of hair, still mostly dark and cut short; gray eyes set in a pleasantly weathered face; and a blue-and-brown plaid shirt. "Good morning," I began brightly.

His lips stretched slightly into the hint of a smile. He nodded, almost imperceptibly.

"You from around here?" I asked.

A pause. His tongue wet his upper lip. He took in a breath and let it out. "Wisconsin," he enunciated quietly, with a tilt of his head toward the east.

"Do you have family?"

"My wife died."

"I'm sorry."

He shrugged. His tongue worked all around his lips, and then he wiped his mouth with the back of his hand. "We never had kids," he said. "My niece looks after me."

"Uh-huh." I nodded. "What kind of work did you do?"

"Farming. Dairy cows, mostly."

"My dad was a dairy farmer," I said.

He smiled, his gray eyes twinkling.

Pretty normal stuff. Similar to scores of conversations I'd had in nursing homes.

However, during the exchange I had become aware that the man on my right was listening with extreme interest. He was leaning forward, wide-eyed, mouth slightly open, focused like a hunting dog on point.

Finally, he couldn't stand it any longer. Nodding toward the man across the table, he said to me, "In seven years, I've never once heard that guy speak a word."

It was my turn to be rendered silent.

Seven years! For a moment I had to bow my head, and I looked down at my silly purple shoes.

Whatever had kept this man behind a wall of self-imposed silence—grief, loneliness, illness—the wall had suddenly melted. Not through the ministrations of a therapist or a physician.

Or a pastor.

But simply by being in the presence of a clown, a holy fool.

WOULD WE

Do

IT AGAIN?

ON MARRIAGE

I was a weird kid.

No, I didn't have seventeen imaginary friends, or eat my boogers, or speak in a British accent for a year like my nephew did when he was eight, or carry a briefcase to third grade. (Okay, maybe I *did* have a briefcase; that one is ringing a little bell.)

On the whole, however, I think I was a pretty normal boy—*except* for the fact I thought it would be fun to get married and have kids when I grew up. All of the other boys in my elementary school made horrible faces at the thought of marriage and parenting: "*Yuck!*"

I, on the other hand, thought, "My dad seems pretty happy to be married and have kids. Why wouldn't I want to do that?"

Plus, by fourth grade, I was hopelessly in love with one of my classmates.

Fifteen years later, I married her. We had dated off and on since ninth grade. The six months after our wedding were wonderful. Life was great! I was loving my first call as a pastor. The little riverside town we were in was adorable, not too big and not too small, not too close to our parents and not too far away. We had bought our first house (with thirty-six dollars left over, until our next paychecks, after we made that 5 percent down payment). I was married to the girl of my dreams. I felt like the luckiest guy alive.

Over the next three years, things steadily grew less great. We both tried hard to save our marriage. Lots of therapy. Lots of prayer.

Eventually, the word *divorce* came up in our conversations. More than thirty-five years later, just typing that makes me short of breath. Divorce. "The Big D." I couldn't imagine anything worse. Remember, I was the kid who had wanted to be married since he was nine years old!

I was not only personally devastated at the dying of our relationship; I was concerned about its effect on others. I felt a divorce would be a bad example to the kids in my youth group. (Heck, my wedding ring had a cross engraved on it—I was disappointing God!)

And I couldn't imagine telling my folks. Their own marriage was such a source of joy and comfort and contentment to them. They deeply wished the same for their kids. This would absolutely break their hearts, especially that of my tenderhearted dad.

Dad was in his eighties and very sick during this time, in and out of the hospital, and I thought I would just stick it out until after he died. And I did hang in there, month after miserable month. But he didn't die. Finally, four and a half years after our blissful beginning, there was nothing for my wife and me to do but call it quits.

When I went to tell my parents we were divorcing, I plotted ahead of time how to say it. Could I make the news sound less than outrageously bad, perhaps even a tad hopeful?

I began with an analogy: "When you're sick and you have surgery," I said, "first you feel even worse than you already were. Then, after a while, you get over the chronic illness and start to get better. But if you don't have the surgery, you never get better . . ."

I paused to note the wide-eyed, stricken look on my mother's face. I couldn't look at my dad at all. I took a breath and hurried on: "All this is by way of saying Kathy and I are getting a divorce."

"Oh, thank heavens!" my mother cried. "I thought you were telling us you had cancer!"

I felt like responding, "Oh, I would *much* rather have cancer, even *terminal* cancer, than go through this divorce." I really felt that way. Death at least wouldn't be a disappointment, embarrassing. A failure.

My mom had had a sense for a while that things in my marriage weren't good. But my father—the person who had shown me how happy a good marriage and loving family could make a man—my father may not have had that sense. In any case, any relief he might have felt upon discovering I was not dying was considerably more subdued than my mother's.

When I gave them the news, he was leaning back in his recliner in their living room. Wordlessly, he pulled out his white handkerchief, unfolded it, laid it over his face, returned his arms to his sides . . . and began to weep. When I left some minutes later, he was still lying back in his chair and sobbing under the handkerchief.

I was a weird boy when it came to thinking about marriage; turns out I was also a weird man when it came to *re*marriage. The vast majority of youngish (and sometimes not-so-youngish) heterosexual men whose marriages end, through either divorce or death, remarry very quickly, often within a year. Most men are so female-dependent it's laughable.

The image of my father crying at the news of my divorce stayed with me. For a variety of reasons—most likely including this one—I stayed single for five and a half years. I wanted to do everything I could to get it right.

My second wife, Kris, and I have now been happily married for over thirty years. In hindsight, I'm glad I didn't have terminal cancer back when I was twenty-nine.

About ten years into our marriage, we were at a dinner party with some of our closest friends, six other couples. The host said to the group, "I would be very curious to know what attracted each of you to your spouse."

"Her legs."

"His sports car."

"Her smile."

I was utterly astounded at how superficial all the answers were. These were highly educated, progressive people giving one politically incorrect answer after another.

I continued the trend: "Her sparkly eyes . . . and before we were married, she laughed at my jokes."

The responses continued.

"His mustache."

"Her curves."

"His hair."

Finally, only my spouse was left to answer. All eyes focused on her. Deadly earnest, my dear wife said, "What first attracted me to Bill . . . was his . . . theology."

The crowd erupted in uproarious laughter. All eyes turned to me now, and I reddened.

My theology? My *theology*! Heck, back when we were dating, I had tremendous legs!

One reason facing a divorce at twenty-nine was so difficult for me? Divorce was something that happened only to other people, to other families.

The experience of going through it made me realize I had always been fairly judgmental—no, *significantly* and *un*fairly judgmental—about people who were divorced, especially Christians. I had always thought, "If you just work on things, get counseling, compromise, and communicate, you can get through whatever bumps in the road you encounter. Just hang in there; you can make it."

My first wife and I had done all of those things. So maybe it's not that simple.

Now, I might not be the sharpest knife in the chandelier, but it began to occur to me that maybe I ought to start digging up and weeding out my other prejudices so I might not have to experience them personally in order to see them for what they were.

Ultimately, I have concluded the divorce made me a better person. This and numerous other experiences over the past few decades have taught me, "Never say never." Failing at marriage made me humbler. And more gentle.

It made me a better pastor.

My sister was about to marry a twice-divorced man. Our mother was apoplectic! "Twice he's been divorced! There's no way this will last!" I admit I was concerned, but I was not hysterical. Well, my sister went ahead and got married (of course). About six months later, at age thirty-five, she suffered a brain aneurysm. It miraculously didn't kill her, but she was permanently "a bit out of plumb," as her husband, Tony, so graciously put it. He patiently cared for her for the next thirty years, until her death.

My brothers and I call him *St. Anthony*.

On Valentine's Day a dozen years ago, I had the privilege of officiating at the marriage-renewal vows of a dozen couples who had been married fifty years or more. Among them was a pair that had been married for eighty years! These two were ninety-eight and ninety-six, still very sharp, and living independently in their own house. (At one point, the husband was asked the secret of their long and presumably happy marriage. "Listen to your wife's suggestions . . . and do 'em!" Not bad advice. Clearly, he's the expert.)

Two of their kids were also at the ceremony with their spouses, and the *kids* had each been married nearly sixty years. Imagine being married nearly sixty years and with both of your parents still alive!

At the ceremony, I couldn't help but think about my own parents, who were married for forty-six years, until my father died at age eighty-one. Mom was left a widow at only sixty-five.

A year or two after my dad died, I encouraged my mom to date again if she wanted to do so.

"Oh, no! No one could ever compare to your dad," she said.

"Well, that may be true," I replied. "But Dad isn't one of the options anymore. Your choices are some nice man or being lonely. I just want you to know that us kids are entirely supportive if you want to date or even marry again."

We had this conversation every few years. Finally, after more than ten years of widowhood, Mom reported over the phone from her winter home in Arizona that she had a gentleman friend. I was so happy for her.

Soon there was talk of a second man—in *addition* to the first. Then a third contender entered the picture!

My wife and kids and I were about to visit Mom for our annual winter getaway, and I couldn't wait to meet these three guys. I was busting with curiosity. What did they look like? How old were they? Where had they lived before Arizona? How did their kids feel about their dating? How did Mom successfully juggle three guys at once? Did they know about each other?

But six days before we were to arrive, Mom died of a heart attack.

I'm grateful she had the companionship of these men. Looking back, though, I can't help but think that perhaps at age seventy-seven, she should have limited herself to dating no more than two guys at a time.

In 2013, the Minnesota State Legislature was considering a bill to make same-sex marriage legal. As you can imagine, a lot of pastors were campaigning against this bill. My wife and I worked hard in support of it, and I was asked as a clergyperson to testify in favor of the bill.

Thinking of everything I had experienced regarding love and marriage, and everything my family had experienced, I gave this testimony:

> My younger brother John and I were extremely close growing up. I was so excited when he and his wife started having children. I didn't have any of my own yet. I loved being an uncle. Claire and Jim grew up in the church I now serve. A couple of great kids! Claire grew up, fell in love with a wonderful man, and, three years ago, married him.
>
> Jim grew up and is now a senior in college, on the dean's list; but when he falls in love, he will not be able to marry the one he loves. By the time Jim was three or four years old, I was very sure that he was gay. Jim didn't choose to be gay. I didn't choose to be straight. Why shouldn't Jim be able to share the same right to marriage as his sister does? I have had the deep honor of officiating at the weddings of four of my nieces. Current state law infringes on my freedom of religion by prohibiting me to officiate at Jim's marriage.
>
> One comic has said, "Let gays marry. Why shouldn't they be as miserable as the rest of us?" That may (or may not) be kind of a funny line. But I'm not miserable. My marriage

means the world to me. Next month, my wife and I will celebrate our twenty-fifth wedding anniversary. My marriage is a place of safety, welcome, commitment, companionship, intimacy, trust.

Yes, all of that can happen without marriage. But our relationship is acknowledged, encouraged, and celebrated by the world and by the Church. Why should Jim be excluded from that acknowledgment, encouragement, and celebration because of the way God made him?

Marriage says "We are family" in a way no other word does.

(The legislature made same-sex marriage legal that year.)

I GUESS WE MADE OUR POINT

My gay friends have told me that one of the most painful aspects of coming out is disappointing their parents, shattering their hopes and dreams. Hopes of their child being part of the typical American Dream—husband, wife, 2.1 kids, house, yard, and white picket fence.

My spouse, Kris, and I were very intentional about trying not to place those expectations on our kids, especially the presumption of *husband/wife*, in case any or all of them turned out to be gay. We—especially my wife—were careful, when speaking of the future, not to say to our son, "Someday, if you get married, you and your wife . . ." or to our girls, "Someday, if you get married, you and your husband . . ." Instead, we would say, "In the future, if you and your boyfriend or girlfriend . . ." From their earliest days of childhood, we wanted to be explicit that it was fine by us if they were attracted to people of the same sex.

One day, when our youngest was fourteen, Kris started to say to her, "Someday, perhaps, you and your boyfriend or girlfriend—"

Our other daughter, eighteen years old at the time, interrupted. "Mom!" she said sharply. "I know it's a great disappointment to you . . . but it looks like all your children are straight."

The Encouraging Spouse

How can you tell if a person needs encouragement?
If he's still breathing!

—S. Truett Cathy

An old story about a long-married couple, a pastor and his wife, goes like this: one week the pastor mentions to his wife that he thinks he will preach about sex this week.

"Oh, my," replies his wife, "do you think that's wise?" A silence follows. "I *really* don't think that's a good idea, dear," she insists. "Will you please reconsider?"

Crestfallen, her husband reluctantly agrees. After a few moments of thought, he smiles and says, "All right. I'll preach about sailing then!"

"*Sailing?*" his wife thinks. "Why sailing? What's gotten into him? . . . Ah, well, at least it's not *sex!*" So she says nothing to discourage him.

Come Sunday morning, the pastor's wife is sick with a cold and fever, and she informs her husband she will not be attending worship that day.

The pastor tells his wife to rest up.

Then he gets to thinking: "If she isn't going to be there, I think I *will* preach about sex." And he does. He decides, however, not to tell his wife. No need to upset her.

A few days later, his wife has recovered sufficiently to be out doing her weekly shopping. At the grocery store, she runs into a couple of women from the parish, who rush up and delightedly exclaim, "Oh, we are so glad you're feeling better. It was a shame you had to miss services on Sunday. We were just saying we thought it was one of your husband's best sermons ever!"

Puzzled, the pastor's wife replies, "Really? Well, that is so surprising. I don't know why he thinks he's such an expert on the subject. He's only tried it twice . . . and he threw up both times."

I once heard a pastor who had been a moderator of the Presbyterian Church (a moderator is something like a national bishop who serves a two-year term) tell about a time he and his spouse were given a tour of a very large Presbyterian church building. As their host led them into the massive sanctuary, the moderator couldn't help but let out a low whistle.

He was a gifted and well-known minister himself, known primarily for his courageous leadership on social justice issues. He had led medium-sized congregations but had never pastored a big, grand church like this one.

He gaped at the magnificent stained-glass windows, painting the pews with colored light from the afternoon sun. Turning around and lifting his gaze to the balcony, he saw the massive organ pipes standing like sentinels before a giant's drawbridge and enough pews for the two-hundred-voice choir.

Then he looked at the pulpit. He pointed at it and lifted his eyebrows. "May I?" he asked his host.

"Go right ahead."

The pastor climbed the eight steps to the chancel. Three more steps brought him into that marvelous hand-carved oaken pulpit. He put his hands on either side of the lectern and looked out at the fifteen hundred seats, up to the balcony, back to the main floor, left and right, imagining himself preaching to such a crowd.

Then he shook his head and said to his wife, "I could never fill this place."

"True," she agreed. "But I bet you could empty it."

(Courageous stands for social justice have a way of doing that.)

My parishioners think the worst thing for a pastor is to get to Saturday night and the sermon still isn't done. But I tell them there's something even worse: to get to Saturday night and the sermon *is* done . . . but it's lousy. That's when you think, "Boy, I hope the music is good tomorrow."

I *try* to finish the Sunday sermon by Thursday noon. But it's rare that this miracle actually happens. More often it's Saturday noon before I've put the finishing touches on my sermon, and occasionally it's later. One Saturday night at about nine o'clock, I got up from the desk in my home study and reported to my spouse, who was relaxing with a book, "Well, I *finally* got my sermon done. Frankly, I think it's pretty darn good . . . a little long, though."

Without looking up from her book, she responded, "Well, it's either one or the other."

ON LUCK

After many months—and thousands of dollars' worth—of marriage counseling, my first wife and I finally ended our marriage. It was extraordinarily painful for both of us.

For the most part, the congregation I was serving at the time was extremely gracious, especially since it was the 1980s, when divorce was less common among clergy than it is today. But that graciousness didn't change the fact that I had failed at the most important thing in my life. On top of the personal pain, I was incredibly embarrassed. I really didn't want to talk about it with anyone, certainly not with my parishioners.

Unfortunately, my parishioners didn't always feel the same way. Many of them couldn't help but provide sincere, well-meaning comments: "Mary and I have learned that it takes communication above all things" or "Ralph and I committed to never going to bed angry." That sort of thing. Well intended. Not terribly helpful.

A couple of months after I announced our impending divorce to the congregation, I was visiting a parishioner in the hospital. He was a regular Sunday worshipper but a quiet guy with whom I had not become very well acquainted. Our talk at the hospital was probably our first one-on-one conversation without his more outgoing wife and kids around.

Within a few minutes of my arrival, Arlen said, "You know, Bill, I haven't had the chance to tell you how sorry I am about your divorce. That must be so hard."

"Thanks. It is really hard."

"You know, Kitty and I have been married for thirty years. And it's been a really good marriage."

And then, wait for it: "You know what the key to our success is?" Arlen looked up at me from his hospital bed. "Hoo boy," I thought, looking back at him, "here it comes. What will it be this time—'compromise,' 'hard work,' 'forgiveness,' the ever-popular 'communication'?"

I waited silently.

"Luck!" he said forcefully. "Just plain dumb luck!"

I could have kissed him . . . on the lips! This was such a word of grace to me that I almost burst into tears. Thank you, Arlen.

He died unexpectedly a few days later, at age sixty. I am forever grateful to him.

A famous psychologist tells the true story of a family consisting of a mom and dad and three highly successful teenage children. All three of these teens were excellent students, leaders in school and church, good athletes and musicians, simply all-around all-American kids. Someone from their local church, noting what wonderful children these parents had raised, asked the couple if they would be willing to teach a little class on parenting at church, to share the secrets of their success.

"Oh, gosh, we're not parenting experts or anything," they replied. "We don't have any special training."

"Well, you can't argue with success," the inquirer replied. "Just share what sorts of things you did and how they worked."

Reluctantly, the couple agreed. They put together some ideas and presented a four-week class in their local church.

The class was very well received, and word spread. The couple was asked to come and share their insights with other congregations. The couple was hesitant, but they finally agreed. Soon they were "experts" being flown all over the country to share with other parents how they had raised such prize-winning children.

Then, lo and behold, the mother of these three teenagers became pregnant. Soon the couple was in the diaper business once again, after a long layoff. And as this child grew older, it became clear he would be one of those "challenging" children. He was disobedient to his parents, got in trouble at school, and eventually ran afoul of the law. All of the tricks of the parenting trade that had worked so well with the first three children were absolutely useless with this fourth one.

And the parents said: "We have come to realize we actually know nothing about parenting. That the first three kids turned out so well was nothing but dumb luck!"

They stopped offering parenting classes.

Like Arlen's words to me, this story is a word of grace to so many parents. We all do the best we can. Of course we do. But how the kids turn out is, to a huge and frightening extent, like so many other things—outside of our control. And sometimes, I believe, outside of their control.

Luck.

A few years ago, in a sermon, I mentioned a recently published study about the significant role luck plays in business success. It was not at all the main point of the sermon or even in my manuscript. I had thrown it in rather offhandedly at the last second.

But what a reaction it provoked from several of the successful businessmen and women in the congregation! "Luck?" they cried, confronting me after the service. "Luck! We make our own luck in this world! It's called *hard work*! Luck has nothing to do with success in business!"

I was shocked. I hadn't received this strong of a critical reaction even to my most recent sermons on peacemaking or homosexuality.

To one long-retired businessman who was fuming at me, I responded calmly, "Well, I was just quoting the study, but it does seem reasonable to me. For example, my younger brother was highly successful in business until this Great Recession hit. Now he's having a tough time."

The parishioner snorted. "Well, then, he's not a very good businessman, is he?"

Luck.

(Some years later I learned that no less a successful businessman than Warren Buffett attributed most of his success to luck. He called it "winning the ovarian lottery," being born into a wonderful family and having good opportunities. Dang! I wish I had known that during this conversation with my parishioner.)

Speaking of the lottery, a good friend of mine tells of occasionally musing about winning the lottery, as so many of us do. Then he took a trip to rural Kenya and realized, "I already won the lottery!" He's returned every year for mission work at a school there and gives a quarter of his income to it. He's embodying the promise and the charge to Abram in the book of Genesis (12:2), in which God promises Abram and Sarai, "I will bless you, and make your name great, *so that* [emphasis mine] you will be a blessing." Dietrich Bonhoeffer said words to this effect: "Blessing does not constitute privileged status; it confers responsibility."

Are you lucky? Pass it on.

On Being a Boy

Male stupidity comes in two main categories.

Category One:

Our twenty-something son recently prepaid for gas inside the station, then got in his car and drove off. About a mile later, it occurred to him he had forgotten to fill his tank! I consoled him by saying, "Andy, I bet some guy does that at least once a week at every gas station in America."

I'm not sure I've ever met a woman who would do such a stupid thing. Or if she did, she would go back to the station like a sensible person to rectify her mistake and get her gas.

My son was too embarrassed to do this.

Do women realize how *difficult* it is to be a male?

(I'm not talking about being one gender or the other *in society*; clearly, women have been on the short end of that stick forever and, tragically, continue to be so. I'm talking about how difficult it is to be a male in everyday life. I don't even need to mention what wimps men are when it comes to pain. I've long contended that if we were the ones having babies, there would only be about 30,000 people on the planet and certainly never a second child in the family.)

Again I ask: do women realize how difficult it is to be a male? Oh, they certainly know how hard it is to live with males, to raise males, to be married to them, to deal with them at work, to care for aging male parents, and so on (and so on). But can they appreciate how difficult it is to actually *be* a boy, of whatever age?

It's a real challenge. We are at a great disadvantage compared to women. You see, that Y chromosome that makes us male gives us more than deep, sexy voices and the ability to tell a Phillips screwdriver from a flathead.

That Y chromosome also gives us the knack to remember Babe Ruth's batting average from 1926 and every fart joke we heard in fourth grade. Unfortunately, filling our heads with such senseless knowledge significantly impedes our facility at remembering things like wedding anniversaries or two out of the three items we were supposed to pick up at the store.

Now, my brother-in-law figured out a surefire way not to miss his wife's birthday, Valentine's Day, or their anniversary anymore. He signed up at the florist to have flowers, with a note from him attached, automatically delivered to his wife on those three days a year. It worked perfectly the first year. But on his wife's next birthday, when he arrived home from work, he noticed the bouquet on the dining table and said, "Nice flowers, honey. Where'd you get 'em?"

I once read the true account of a man who took a memory course in which he learned to picture items in a certain pattern so he could easily recall them later. Soon after completing the course, he was about to leave the house to run some errands when his wife asked him to pick up a few things at the store as long as he was out.

"Now, write these down," she said.

"Oh, I don't need to," he countered confidently. "Just say them slowly and I will remember them."

His wife carefully named six items for him to pick up. "Can you remember that many?"

"Of course!" he exclaimed triumphantly. "Just watch!"

When he returned home about an hour and a half later, his wife asked, "Were you able to remember all the items?"

Silence.

Finally he replied, "Oh, I remember all the items, all right." And then he added sheepishly, "But I forgot to go to the store."

It's hard to be a boy. (And the bitter truth for many men such as myself—those who love, and hate to disappoint, the women in their lives—is accepting that dealing with us or living with us at any age is extremely frustrating and difficult.)

The concept of "emotional labor" was first introduced by an academic, Arlie Hochschild, in her 1983 book *The Managed Heart*. Emotional labor—remembering birthdays, knowing where the spare set of keys is, knowing when the household is low on paper towels and planning to buy more—in most households falls disproportionately on women.

Question: How many teenage boys does it take to change a roll of toilet paper?

Answer: No one knows. It's never been done.

Category Two:

We can't find things. And just why is it that men can never find anything? I have a theory. Scientists tell us the Y chromosome is so tiny it can be seen only under a microscope. Humph! Well, that may be literally true, but let me explain the actual *effect* of the Y chromosome on a man's eyesight. If you make a Y with your fingers and then hold those two fingers vertically so they are just touching your eyelashes, you will have some idea of how hard it is for men to find things.

When my brother was about twelve, he headed to the basement to retrieve something. A few steps down, he stopped and called upstairs: "Mom, you want to just come now or wait until I call you to help me find it?" Based on his experience, he knew he'd never locate the item on his own.

One of my all-time favorite cartoons is of a man standing next to an open refrigerator door. Inside the fridge are a zillion sticks of butter stacked one upon another *and nothing else.* He calls to his wife, "Hon, where's the butter?"

That this hit a nerve is borne out by the fact the cartoon has been published hundreds of times and has been made into a card that decorates thousands (millions?) of refrigerators today.

Maybe our biggest trouble is it's also *fun* to be a boy, even when it hurts.

Literally.

My theory is the Y chromosome not only affects our ability to remember and find things. It also, when combined with testosterone, tells us that doing incredibly stupid things will make us the happiest boys in the world.

When he was in junior high, my friend Steve and his buddies biked to the local lake to go swimming. On their way, they passed a number of their female friends playing soccer. On the boys' return, the girls were still there. Steve's friend, riding just ahead of him, got the brilliant idea to moon the girls. How fun that would be!

So as he rode by, downhill at high speed, he stood on his pedals and with one hand managed to pull down his swimming trunks. Not to be outdone, Steve followed suit. The girls erupted in squealing.

"But, remember," relates Steve, "we had just come from swimming. I couldn't get my suit back up with one hand, so I just sat down buck naked on my bike seat. But since I was wet, my bare keister slid right off the back of the seat . . . and onto my rapidly spinning rear wheel . . ."

It's hard to be a boy.

(And if you are a boy of any age, I guarantee you are squirming in your seat right now.)

I have had many bike adventures of my own. The most serious was also the most recent, just a few years ago, when I was old enough to know better. Way old enough. A bunch of family and friends had gathered on a summer weekend in Colorado for my niece's wedding, which I was to officiate at four o'clock Saturday afternoon at the chalet halfway up the mountain at Breckenridge. That morning, about a half dozen of us fifty-something males decided to go mountain biking at Copper Mountain. We rented bikes and helmets at the base, took the chairlift up to the top, and then zigzagged our way carefully and safely down the switchbacks. At the bottom someone said, "Wow, that was fun! Let's do it again." I was a little reluctant to tempt fate once more. After all, I had important responsibilities in a few hours, but . . . peer pressure.

And testosterone.

(A little aside here about the effects of testosterone. They are real! A friend of mine is a transgender male; he began life as a female. About ten years ago, he started undergoing hormone therapy to transition. He reports it made him "crazy . . . I was aggressive and crabby, barely human. I had to cut back on the dosage." Another female-to-male transgender person I know of reported thinking, while getting blasted with testosterone, "I don't know how men even manage to function—there are so many crazy impulses going on in my brain now.")

As we all know, most teenage boys are indeed "barely human." And to some extent, men of any age deal with the challenge of testosterone constantly. For example . . .

Back to Copper Mountain. Proceeding down a different route this time, my buddies and I came to a "trick" apparatus that had been constructed along the trail: a narrow boardwalk about thirty feet long with a teeter-totter sort of device in the middle. You rode up the teeter-totter, and as you crossed the center of it, your weight caused it to go down on the other side. You came down on the far side, then onto the boardwalk, then onto the trail once more. The high side of the mountain was to our left, the low side to our right.

One of our guys took a turn at it, but he didn't even make it up the first half of the teeter-totter. He lost his balance and tottered off to the left (fortunately the high side) and into the soft earth next to the trail.

Well, I could see the problem. Jerry obviously hadn't gone fast enough. Wanting to impress my friends, to show them and myself I was still a master biker, and, of course, with testosterone clouding my judgment, I thought I'd take a run at it . . .

With a deep breath I bombed down the trail, onto the boardwalk, up the teeter-totter, down the other side of the teeter-totter—yes! I did it!—but then I immediately started to lose control. I veered off the side of that narrow boardwalk into midair. To the *right,* the *low* side of the trail! I didn't even get my hands out to brace myself before I fell at least six feet headfirst into the ground.

I felt—and heard!—my neck snap. A blinding flash of light exploded in my brain, and my diaphragm expelled every bit of air from my lungs and from anywhere else in my body a molecule of oxygen might have been hiding.

I lay on my back, dazed and disoriented. After a few seconds I tried to wiggle my toes. They moved! Same with my fingers. *That* was a relief. If I could ever breathe again, I would check out the rest of my body.

I opened my eyes. The stunned and horrified faces of my comrades didn't give me reassurance. One whipped out his phone. "I'm calling the chopper."

I waggled a hand back and forth and then, still not able to get a breath, managed a croaky, "Not yet."

Meanwhile, I was also thinking to myself, "You simply can't die . . . not until tomorrow. You'll ruin Katie's wedding if you die today." (I may be an idiot, but I'm a thoughtful idiot.)

In a few minutes I regained my ability to breathe. So, despite a sore back and neck and an abrasion across my forehead from the helmet (now cracked), I was able to ride—albeit slowly—the rest of the way down the mountain.

And perform the wedding.

A few days later, back in Minnesota, I went to the doctor and discovered I had indeed broken a vertebra. Trying to salvage some dignity (at least it was a male doc, who could understand these things), I said, "I *was* wearing a helmet."

"Oh, I know," replied my physician. "Otherwise you wouldn't be here today."

To this day, when I am tired or have been exercising a lot, my back will hurt where I fractured the vertebra. I don't complain. Instead, I think of it as a little warning light on the dashboard of life: "Don't be an idiot."

Sometimes the only person a man has around to impress is himself. My friend Andy is a diehard sailor. One evening a couple of years ago, he was sailing back from the Apostle Islands to Superior, Wisconsin. Since he was traveling solo, he was wearing his inflatable life vest. Very smart, for a man.

As he entered the Superior harbor, he started to gather the buoys and fenders needed for docking. I'll let Andy take it from here:

"I was reaching headfirst down into the lazarette, the storage area under the hatch, for one more fender. That compartment is deep. I can fit in it. But the opening isn't large, not much wider than I am."

(*You can do it!* a little voice told him . . .)

"I'm reaching and reaching for that last fender. I'm probably within twenty degrees of being straight upside down. I can al-l-l-l-most reach it when I hear a loud pop! Almost like an explosion. 'What the heck is that?' I thought.

"A second later I feel myself being strangled. My life vest! In my wriggling I must have somehow triggered the automatic inflator. Now expanded, the life vest completely fills the opening and it's still inflating. I'm wedged in there, stuck upside down. There are no handholds. Absolutely nothing with which to push or pull myself free. I can't breathe. It took only a moment for me to imagine the headline: 'Sailboat on autopilot runs aground in Superior harbor. Solo sailor found asphyxiated, trapped upside down in the hatch.'

"Starting to lose consciousness, I knew I had only one last desperation shot before I choked to death. To this day I don't really know what I did, but I made one last effort and somehow freed myself.

"As I lay there gasping, I thought, 'That was stupid.'"

Addendum from the author: Not being a sailor myself, I didn't know that term *lazarette*, so I looked it up. Turns out it comes from the biblical story of Lazarus, whom Jesus raised from the dead. On the old sailing ships, the lazarette was a below-deck compartment used to store the bodies of important passengers or crew members who had died on the voyage.

How very nearly applicable in this case!

The list goes on and on. I know of a man who lost his fingers up to the first knuckle trying to prove one could trim a hedge with a lawn mower.

On a dare from other boys, lads will try most anything imaginable. Back in high school, my friend Kenny got in a contest with a classmate to see who could swallow the most minnows. The friend gave up when the number reached 120! Both boys shortly thereafter puked up the minnows, most of which were still flopping around. While bored on a fishing trip, my ten-year-old nephew asked if any of the other boys would give him ten bucks to swallow a leech.

He got the ten. I'd say he earned it.

Another friend of mine, Tom, tells of a long day spent fishing with a couple of his buddies, back when they were in their early twenties. They had not had a nibble all day long. In desperation, one of his friends started rummaging around in his tackle box and pulled out a garish-looking combo of feathers and spinners that resembled nothing in nature, and started to tie it to his line. Tom looked at it in amazement and said, "Oh my gosh! If you catch something on that god-awful lure, I'll bite its head off!"

First cast, his friend caught a crappie. Like Herod after Salome's dance, Tom had to follow through on his promise. (I think there may have been some alcohol involved in this incident, which would have helped.)

The most horrifying youth worker story I've heard—and I've heard a lot—was of a Young Life mentor who got caught up in the fun of helping one of his teenage charges scare his girlfriend by "pretending" they were going to launch a toboggan off an icy ski jump. Then somehow they all managed to let go of the sides of the jump at the same time, and indeed, they found themselves racing down the ski jump *on a toboggan!* The girl had the good sense to faint dead away, and so when she hit the pile of snow at the bottom she was entirely limp and was unhurt. The other three participants (males) had numerous broken bones. The Young Life leader had the brilliant idea of bracing himself with his arms extended straight out.

He had to be flown from New England to a Chicago hospital to have his arms pulled back out of his shoulder sockets. (Who knew a hospital would specialize in such a thing?)

I could fill an entire book with examples of this type of male stupidity. But it's already been done. In fact, to date there are at least nine Darwin Awards books, plus thousands of other examples on their website. You might have heard of them. The sole criterion for the awards? You can probably guess:

"In the spirit of Charles Darwin, the Darwin Awards commemorate individuals who protect our gene pool by making the ultimate sacrifice of their own lives. Darwin Award winners eliminate themselves in an extraordinarily idiotic manner, thereby improving our species' chances of long-term survival."

The books list one idiotic experience after another, experiences that resulted in the death (or occasionally, and always painfully, self-sterilization) of the subject.

Note that being male is *not* a criterion. However, a few years ago it was reported that "scientists were surprised to discover that 90 percent of the Darwin Awards winners were male."

What? Surprised? I'm absolutely *shocked!*

That the figure wasn't 99 percent.

Or higher.

It's hard to be a boy.

ON TIME

onfession time: I wear a watch when I'm camping in the
wilderness.
I know; that's pathetic.

What I tell my camping buddies is this: I fear that on a cloudy
day, when I can't see the sun to get a rough estimate of the time, if
I didn't wear my watch I would eat all three of the day's meals by
midmorning. Actually, I just really like to know the time. Probably some sort of control thing, so I can make plans. Okay, *definitely* some sort of control thing. Though I'm not quite as bad as one of
my friends who claims she likes "to plan [her] spontaneity"—but
I'm close.

In some families, "cleanliness is next to godliness." (My sister-
in-law says that in her house, "cleanliness is next to impossible.")
But when I was growing up, the unspoken rule in our house was
"*promptness* is next to godliness" in the hierarchy of family values.
Being prompt meant you respected the other person's time and
valued the other person. (And promptness meant you didn't have
to walk to school because you missed the bus. Mom wasn't going
to drive us when it was our own darn fault.)

Second confession: I like having deadlines for projects. Not surprising, I suppose, given the watch-in-the-wilderness story. Certainly my fondness for deadlines has something to do with the delight I take in crossing things off my to-do list. I'm one of those people who writes things on my to-do list that I've already done, just so I can cross them off. I know . . . sad.

Deadline.

Turns out, the origin of the word is awfully interesting, equal parts *interesting* and *awful.* Several sources assert it comes from the American Civil War, specifically the Andersonville prison camp, where captured Union soldiers were imprisoned by the Confederacy. There was a railing twenty feet in from the wall of the stockade to warn inmates to go no farther. If you crossed that line, the guards would shoot. It became known as the *dead line.*

So, do I like deadlines because they remind me that someday I will be dead?

Carpe diem—seize the day!

Speaking of seizing the day, we are well aware that most of the world has a much more relaxed view of time than Euro-Americans do.

While visiting my brother-in-law, a doctor in Tanzania, I one day asked him what the Swahili word for *white person* is. The answer was *mzungu.* But then he quickly added, "Interestingly enough, it doesn't literally signify skin color. It just has come to refer to Europeans or Americans, regardless of color. It actually comes from the word *mzungaro,* meaning *circle.* Seeing my confused look, he continued, with a wry smile, "A *mzungu* is literally 'one who runs around in circles.'"

Ouch.

I refer to my own sense of time as "uptight white guy" time, or "pale male time."

In honor of my late mother, I try hard to be on time. Supper in our house when I was growing up was at 6:00.

Not 5:58. And certainly not 6:01. "Be there or be square?" No, "Be there or be hungry." No one waited for you.

Thus, being late makes me anxious, and as one of my parishioners put it, "I'd rather be a little early than a little stressed."

A few years ago, I officiated a wedding between a young woman from Ghana and a young man from the Virgin Islands. The groom and his family have the pale skin of European descent but a fully "island time" sense of punctuality.

Knowing that both families had an extremely relaxed sense of promptness, the couple set the time of their wedding rehearsal for 6:00 p.m. on Friday but told everyone in their wedding party the start time was 5:00 p.m. At six o'clock those present for the start of the rehearsal were the couple, the soloist, the wedding coordinator, and (of course) me. Not a single family member from either side of the family. By seven, a full *two hours* after the time they were told to arrive, enough of the wedding party had shown up that we could limp through a rehearsal. The maid of honor, the bride's sister, showed up at 7:20.

The wedding on the following day followed a pretty similar pattern. The limo bringing the men of the wedding party showed up twenty minutes after the start time of the wedding.

The wedding coordinator was losing her mind. But I had fairly successfully adopted a "when in Rome" attitude and just figured, "We'll start when we start and we'll finish when we finish." (The flower girl never did show up. Good thing we didn't wait for her.)

Well, we got the couple married and they are now the parents of two wonderful children. Not a punctual family, mind you, but perfectly delightful. I greatly admire them. I am jealous of their attitude about time. I am quite proud of myself for, during that one weekend, successfully adopting a relaxed attitude about time, but just writing these past few paragraphs makes me tense again.

Like most people I know, I always feel short of time, rushed, tense. Too many things to do in too short of a time. For years I met with a spiritual director on a monthly basis, and invariably that frustration of mine came up in conversation. John would listen patiently, tilt his head slightly, give a gentle half-smile and ask quietly, "What is on your to-do list that God didn't put there?" What an insightful question. Month after month I couldn't come up with a good answer.

Finally the solution dawned on me.

I switched spiritual directors.

I once attended a seminar on effective time management. About 200 people had preregistered—and prepaid—for the seminar. But a full one-third of the registrants failed to show up. I presume because of a lack of time. The woman seated next to me was the administrative assistant to a guy who had signed up, but when the day came he couldn't find the time to go, so he sent her in his place with instructions to train him when she got back to the office. I bet he never made time to talk to her about it.

The most memorable time-management tip I've heard was how in one company the managers agreed that if someone's office door was closed, the rule was you did not knock on the door to interrupt them. But if you *really* needed to consult with them right away, you *could* knock on the door . . . if you were willing to fork over twenty bucks out of your own pocket. I like that.

Still, I believe we are not thinking big enough when we talk about time management. We don't need little tips. We need a paradigm shift. We need to think outside the box. We need a new business intelligence strategy. We need data wrangling and augmented analytics! We need every buzzword on the bleeding edge of the core competency toolbox.

No.

We simply need a new calendar. I mean *an entirely new calendar*. I first read of this general idea decades ago, so long ago that I cannot now locate any reference to it on the internet. So, while I would like to, I can't give credit to the person who came up with the germ of the idea.

Actually, the real germ of the idea goes back to the French Revolution. In an effort to be more efficient, a ten-day week was established. Called the French Republican calendar, it was in use from 1793 to 1805. The idea was to work nine straight days and then have a day off.

Did this social experiment have to be abandoned because the workers revolted? No. Then why? Because the horses kept dying! Horses are not made to be worked nine straight days. Neither are humans, hence the term *Sabbath*, referring to the day of rest on the seventh day following six days of work.

The institution of the forty-hour workweek gave workers two days off in every week of seven days. A welcome and healthy improvement for those able to follow that schedule.

But my calendar? My calendar would consist of nine-day weeks: four weeks per month, thus thirty-six days per month. Every month. Ten months per year. Yes, math wizards, I know that means five days are left over (and every fourth year, six days are left over). We'll come back to that.

What are the advantages of this? I'm thinking most people would work six days and then have three days off. Think of it: that coveted "three-day weekend" would come *every* week! Or, people might do three days of work, then a day off, then three more days of work, followed by two days off. Either way, each week we would get six days of work and three days off, which means 33 percent of the week we are not working, compared to the current 28 percent. I don't know about you, but virtually every week I think, "If I just had one more day here, I could get my work done," and certainly every weekend I think, "One more day off sure would be nice." Don't you?

"But how do we get the work done?" you are wondering. (If you're an uptight guy like me.)

Easy: fewer meetings.

Things you need to do weekly (attending staff meetings, doing laundry, flossing your teeth, setting out the garbage can, preparing a sermon—yes, and *listening* to a sermon) only come around once every nine days instead of every seven.

Things you need to do monthly (attending monthly meetings, exercising, changing the litter box) only come around once every thirty-six days instead of every thirty . . . or thirty-one . . . or twenty-eight.

Which brings me to the next advantage of this concept. With this calendar, the days of the week will fall on the same dates each month. If the third of the month is a Tuesday this month, it's a Tuesday every month. Easy to remember. If your wedding was on a Saturday, your anniversary is always on a Saturday. And while we are at it, let's arrange this calendar so Christmas is not on a weekend (a real drag for clergy).

Now, back to those extra days. In the first place, we'll put them in the summer, not in February, like leap day. For Pete's sake! Whoever thought that up obviously didn't live in Minnesota. Second, I figure those extra five days are holidays for all. (Can I get an "amen!" here?) Okay, those who *have* to work over these five days of national holiday—nurses, police officers, lifeguards, ice-cream vendors—will get double time *and* comp time.

Personally, I think this is one of my best ideas yet. However, when I shared it with my mother a few years back, she gave me a baleful look, slowly shook her head, and muttered:

"It's obvious that you already have too much time on your hands."

On Unconditional Love

One of the joys of being a parish pastor is that, along with attending to the mundane tasks of church life—fixing a leaky urinal, negotiating between groups arguing over whose responsibility it is to make the Sunday morning coffee, deciding which bulletin cover to use for Easter Sunday—one also gets to wrestle with the *big ideas*. Ideas like God. And love. Suffering. Grace.

Even "What is the meaning of life?" You get the picture.

When I was in seminary, I once heard a parish pastor say, "You can't really be an effective pastor until you're at least thirty-five years old. You just don't have enough life experience until then."

I found the comment disturbing. At the time, I was eleven years shy of that figure and but a few months away from graduation. What was I supposed to do until I was thirty-five? Sell Amway and gather life experience? Well, I was ordained and went ahead and served as a pastor, beginning at the oh-so-tender age of twenty-four.

But looking back from the perspective of forty years in ministry, I can see the wisdom of the comment.

For example, after ten years as a parish pastor, I had preached many times about one of the "big ideas": God's unconditional love for us. I understood the concept intellectually. But now I realize I actually had no idea, absolutely no idea . . . until the life-transforming experience of becoming a parent. (I trust many of you who are not parents are more perceptive than I was; this was just my experience.)

I love my spouse, Kris, with all my heart. But I fell in love with her in the first place because she treated me, and continues to treat me, wonderfully.

It's not like that with kids.

Our firstborn, Andy, like his sisters, is today a wonderful human being. He's compassionate, polite, talented, a good worker. I am so proud to be his dad for a lot of reasons.

But things didn't start out that way.

I had wanted to be a dad for a long time, so I was delighted when we learned Kris was pregnant.

Now, a lot of pregnant women have morning sickness for a few hours in the early part of the day, and it lasts maybe a month or two. Kris experienced nausea and vomiting at any and all hours of the day—for seven months of her pregnancy. It seemed every three minutes one could hear the sound of puking.

This awful pregnancy was followed by a normal delivery.

Of course, by *normal* I mean *unbelievably horrible!* Andy was eight and a half pounds; eight of it was his head. I didn't know my wife even *knew* those words, let alone that she would direct them at me.

Andy turned out to be one of those babies that spits up all the time. And he pooped *all* the time. We never changed a diaper that only had pee in it. And these were no ordinary poops. He had explosions. One came just as I was changing him, and I happened to be wearing my best suit at the time. Suddenly I was wearing more than that, as were two walls, the hand-painted curtains, and about eighty square feet of carpet. (Fortunately the carpet was brown in color already).

So. I have a strong memory of holding Andy when he was about two weeks old. Looking at him, I thought back over what he had done for me so far. He had put my beloved Kris through months of discomfort, culminating in twenty-four hours of tortured labor. He had already gone through a zillion diapers. He had cost us thousands of dollars. He kept us up all night, every night. And at two weeks of age, babies don't truly smile, so he had not done *one* positive thing for me.

And yet . . . and yet . . . I loved him. I loved him with a fierceness, and a totality, I had never before even imagined. I could not possibly love anyone or anything more.

As I held my two-week-old son and experienced this incredible sense of love, the light bulb turned on. It dawned on me that this feeling was probably a microcosm of God's infinite and unconditional love for me.

And for you.

Not because of *anything* positive we have done. Simply because of the relationship: parent-child.

Know, dear friend, that you are the cherished child of God.

On Adoption

I grew up with an adopted older sibling. And because of this, adoption seemed normal to me.

My parents married when my father was thirty-four and my mother was eighteen. Yes, quite scandalous. They desired to have children, and finally, after seven years of marriage and a series of miscarriages, a son was born. A second child did not come along—more miscarriages, alas—so five years after my brother's birth, they adopted my sister and thought their family was complete.

Five years later I showed up.

Four years after that my little brother arrived.

If you're doing the math, you know my mom was thirty-nine and my dad was fifty-five when this last child was born. As Dad liked to say, "We had trouble having kids . . . and trouble stopping having kids."

It was not until I was in college that it dawned on me that perhaps I was not a planned pregnancy. My parents confirmed that guess, with my dad quickly adding, "But we like you *now*!"

When my parents were finally done reproducing, they had four kids, a typical family of that day: three brown-haired boys born to them, and a red-headed girl through the gift of adoption.

My parents did a wonderful job of making sure all four of us knew how much we were loved. In their efforts to ensure that Mary wouldn't somehow feel less important than the birth kids, my parents frequently commented about how special Mary was, because "We *chose* her."

So as a young child, I had no idea where *I* came from, but I knew my sister was special. Because of my mom's emphasis on Mary's specialness, I logically concluded she was *more special* than us boys. And this was long before I learned I was an accident.

Jump ahead with me thirty years. As my now-wife and I contemplated our upcoming marriage, we acknowledged we each had some possible fertility issues. But we both said we would be delighted to adopt if we didn't become pregnant. As it turned out, we were able to conceive—about fifteen minutes after we decided to try.

Now, when I was a very young man, I thought it would be a blast to have seven kids—five boys for a basketball team and, just to be fair, a couple of girls for my wife. (I know, I know.)

A few weeks after our first child was born, I came up with a revised number of children for my ideal family . . .

One.

No matter how many times people tell you about how much work kids are, until you have your own, you have no idea.

No idea.

No. Idea . . .

N-O. I-D-E-A.

So I was good with the one all-consuming child we had.

However, my wife really wanted a daughter. And a couple years after we had our firstborn, we were blessed with a girl.

"Thank heavens it was a girl," I thought. "Now we can be done." I loved my kids beyond imagining, but two was plenty.

However, my wife wanted a third child. I was adamantly opposed.

Guess how many we have?

Nonetheless, there were some issues about a third child. As mentioned in the previous essay, the first pregnancy was horrible, as was the second. Each was followed by an excruciating delivery.

Shortly after Kris' second delivery, I said, "Well, honey, I don't know about you, but *I'm* not going through that again." That referring to being in the delivery room with her screaming in agony.

"What do you mean?"

"This is what I mean: If you want to have another baby, fine. But I'm going to play 1950s dad and remain in the waiting room smoking cigarettes." No, I don't normally smoke, and of course, you can't smoke in a hospital, so they would have to be candy cigarettes—I used to love those.

"Or we can adopt," I said.

She didn't need convincing about adoption. In the first place, we are well aware of the effects of global overpopulation. In addition, having a few years earlier seen a UNICEF presentation on the plight of girls in developing nations, we were very enthusiastic about an international adoption.

So for child number three, adoption it would be. For a variety of reasons, India was the country.

My spouse also said to me, "I had the first two. You can do this one."

By *do*, she meant I could do the paperwork. That seemed fair. Over the course of several months, I completed a stack of paperwork over two inches thick, about forty hours of finding legal documents and filling out forms. More than once I thought to myself that my role in conception was *infinitely* more enjoyable than my role in adoption.

Following the completion of the paperwork, we had our home study—our house has never been so clean, before or since—and we passed. (Years later we would attempt to adopt a golden retriever and we *failed* the home inspection, but that's another story.) Now we waited for a match. With two children already, we just didn't feel called to take a child with known disabilities. We requested a healthy baby and one as young as possible, certainly under a year when she would arrive in the US. We knew it would take about six months after our acceptance of a placement before the child would be released to us, so we were asking for a baby six months old or less.

As anyone who has been through it knows, international adoption is a very long and expensive process. It is inevitably accompanied by delays due to bureaucratic snafus, international crises, or demands for bribes. After a year of an excruciating wait, our local adoption agency told us the orphanage in India we had been working through had lost its license for adoption. Had lost it many months earlier. Why didn't someone tell us this before? At any rate, we started over with a new orphanage.

Months later we received the phone call. A child had been selected for us!

Just a couple of minor issues. This child was already eleven months old. And her legs were so flexible the folks in the orphanage weren't sure she would ever walk properly. We had given the adoption agency two conditions. This baby met neither.

But she was a baby waiting for a home. We were parents waiting for a baby.

Hmm. What to do? Well . . . maybe if we saw the photo.

Hah!

Knowing *full well* a glance at a photo would seal the deal, we glanced at the photo. We melted. Huge, shining, bright, black eyes; wavy black hair; chocolate skin, arm reaching out, as if to us. Of course we'll take this baby!

Then began the final waiting.

Month after month of waiting. So much worse than waiting for a birth pregnancy, in which each week you know the baby is getting closer to your arms. You are feeling the baby kick. Mom is getting bigger. (In my case, so was Dad. I'm very empathetic.)

With adoption one is simply waiting. And praying. And waiting. And praying.

Good grief. I felt like I had the teeniest-tiniest sense of how the Jews must have felt waiting and longing for the Messiah for generation after generation. Advent took on new meaning for us.

As we waited for our child and wondered just what this little brown package from India might be like, my spouse and I independently came to the same conclusion: actually, it might be nice to have a kid without our genes.

Finally, we received a date four weeks hence (Advent again). Our daughter Anji (pronounced AHN-jee, the name we had selected) and a six-year-old girl named Malika, to be adopted by another local family, would be coming to the Twin Cities airport, accompanied by a woman named Anita from the orphanage.

After we waited what seemed like four more months, but was actually just the four more weeks, the day finally arrived. Many of our friends wanted to come to the airport with us to greet Anji, but since we already had twenty-seven family members coming, we asked our friends to be patient. The plane was due in from Los Angeles at 4:07 in the afternoon. It was a twenty-five-minute drive to the airport, so just to be sure we'd be there in plenty of time in case we had a flat tire (or three), we left at about 10:30 in the morning. Okay, that's an exaggeration, but not by much. No flat tires, not even one, so we were there way early. This was pre-9/11, so we could assemble right at the arrival gate. In addition to the twenty-seven of us, the other adopting family had perhaps fifteen people, and of course, the gate was crowded with lots of others waiting to welcome regular passengers.

We waited and waited. My brother-in-law video recorded the impatient crowd. He never turned it off during the wait.

It's a long video.

Finally, four o'clock. Wouldn't be long now. We searched the skies for a United Airlines jet.

4:07. No plane rolling into the jetway. 4:15 and no plane. The little kids in our party—expectant siblings and cousins—were literally bouncing off the walls and chairs, and the adults were doing the same thing internally.

4:20 and a United Airlines jet appeared and touched down on the runway ahead of us and turned toward our gate and, indeed, nestled into the jetway. One more interminable wait—perhaps two minutes—and then passengers started disembarking. We were on tiptoe, or little kids on parents' shoulders, many of us standing on chairs. Passenger after passenger disembarked. No Indian woman with two little Indian girls. More passengers. And more passengers, seemingly thousands upon thousands. My gosh, it's like a giant clown car! How many people were on this plane? Los Angeles must be a ghost town now. And then . . .

No more passengers. Thirty seconds went by and no one emerged. Another thirty seconds.

The plane must be empty.

Other than the twenty-seven of us and the fifteen people in the other girl's family, no one was still waiting for arrivals. What in the world? Certainly we would have received word if they had been delayed, wouldn't we? Though given our other experiences with the adoption agency, I wasn't quite confident of that.

Oh, man. I was just starting to ponder what our next step was—I had absolutely no idea—when the Holy Family stepped through the door. Okay, not THE Holy Family, but A Holy Family: Anita, holding our beloved Anji in one arm, with Malika clinging shyly to Anita's side and holding her other hand. Anji was so tiny—seventeen months old and only sixteen pounds—but absolutely gorgeous, with immense black eyes to go with her shiny black hair. And pierced ears! Tears flowed down every cheek in the waiting area, including those of people merely walking by.

Our beautiful daughter! Shy and a bit bewildered, she was unwilling to leave Anita's arms for many minutes. Finally, she consented to go into her new brother's arms, and our family was complete. No words can express our joy.

After a love feast there at the gate, we finally headed home with our little one, firmly, though unhappily, ensconced in her car seat. Anji settled into our family amazingly quickly and happily. It did take her a while to get her days and nights straightened out, but we'd been through that with our first two kids and we were soon in a good rhythm.

Despite the warning we received that she might have trouble walking because of her unusual flexibility, Anji zoomed around our house immediately. And even though she had experienced little English language before arriving, she was able to understand almost everything and was soon talking up a storm in English. Oh, did she talk. Any thought that passed through her head came out her mouth: "Mommy, that dog is big!" "Mommy, can dogs talk to cats?" "Mommy, why do dogs have four legs and we only have two?" "Mommy, can we get a dog?"

A few days after Anji arrived, we discovered she did not come to our house unaccompanied. She had lice. When we mentioned that to our social worker at the adoption agency, she commented, "Oh, yes, that's very common." *Well, you might have mentioned that ahead of time and we could have headed this off at the pass.* As it was, Anji had snuggled in all our beds and been all over the house, so we started in washing loads and loads of clothes and sheets and pillowcases, and we treated every member of the family as if we had lice, just in case.

The recommended treatment at the time was to coat our heads with mayonnaise overnight, wearing shower caps on our heads to keep things relatively clean. The theory was that one night of this should suffocate the lice and the nits. I woke up several times during that night, smelling mayo and convincing myself there must be a turkey sandwich nearby. As I came into full wakefulness, I realized with great disappointment that *I* was the turkey sandwich. (By the way, the mayo worked.)

One evening, a week or two after she arrived, I tiptoed into the girls' shared room and peeked into Anji's crib, where she was sleeping peacefully on her back. By the dim glow of the night-light I could just make out something nestled up by her head. What is that? I reached for it and, to my horror, discovered it was her foot! Her leg was bent entirely straight up, her foot next to her ear! And she was sleeping soundly. Now, that's flexible. Shuddering, I pulled her foot down into a normal position. The thought of it still gives me the willies.

Anji adapted to life in our family with astonishing rapidity. She was nearly constantly smiling and laughing, eager to interact with others, and extraordinarily adorable. She lit up every room she entered.

As Anji grew a bit older, she loved watching the video of the twenty-seven members of the family waiting for her and then the joyous reception over the next half hour when she finally disembarked from the plane. Over the next few years, whenever we asked if she wanted to watch a movie or any family home video, her response was always "Anji video." I mean, she watched it over and over and over. She got to see how very much we all loved her even before she arrived.

One afternoon as the extended family was gathered together, someone observed how happy Anji seemed to be nearly all the time. Her Aunt Lynn responded, not at all in a mean or jealous way, but with some wisdom, "You know, I'd be happy too if every single time I entered a room, all activity and conversation stopped, everyone's face lit up with a giant smile, and people cried in unison, 'lynnnnn!' and rushed over to give me a hug. Yup, I'd be happy too."

How right she is. If everyone on earth were treated with that kind of appreciation, I have to believe there would be instant world peace.

As Anji grew up, each year in our family we observed not only her birthday but three other days the older kids didn't have: her "Gotcha Day," her legal adoption day, and the anniversary of when she became a US citizen at age three. The older kids were understandably jealous of all these celebrations for Anji, similar to my jealousy of how "special" my sister was because my parents *chose* her.

Throughout the adoption process and the long period of waiting, occasionally a niggling thought had flitted through my wife's mind: "Will I be able to love this child as much as our birth children?" As we talked about it then, we noted how before our second child was born, each of us had secretly wondered if we could possibly love this child as much as we adored our first. And then of course, we did, immediately. I assured my wife the same would no doubt hold true with our third child, whether adopted or homegrown. This proved to be gloriously true. As any parent of multiple children knows, one's love doesn't get divided. One's love grows to embrace however many children one has.

As Anji would ride along in the car seat behind me, when it was just the two of us, we had a regular ritual. Anji would say, "Daddy? Do you love me?" And I would answer, "Oh, Anji! yes,

I love you soooooooooooooooooo much!" Over the course of a few years we had done this several hundred times. One day she asked it again, "Daddy, do you love me?" For whatever reason, I responded with an abrupt "no." For a split second I worried about her reaction to my little joke. I needn't have. She flung her head back and laughed and laughed and laughed! She knew that was a *ridiculous* answer. That day and for weeks after she asked me again and again, and I gave the answer "no," and she laughed until she nearly got sick.

What a gift to be that certain of someone else's love.

OUR MIDDLE CHILD

J ust before completing this book, I realized I had an essay about our eldest child and one about our youngest child, but not one about the middle child.

Of course.

I was a middle child. I know what that's like.

When Andy was two, we welcomed a little girl into the family and named her Allison, Allie for short. Growing up with Allie was like having a pint-size Amy Poehler in the house. Hysterically funny, on purpose . . . and not on purpose. And cuter than a kitten on catnip.

When we adopted Anji five years later, it came as both a wonderful gift to Allie . . . and as a kick in the solar plexus. Allie loved Anji immensely and at first sight, but at the same time, she had been replaced as the youngest, was no longer the only girl, and had to share her bedroom. Anji, with her chocolate brown skin, jet-black hair, and sparkly eyes, attracted oohs and aahs everywhere she went. Before, Allie had been the one to elicit those reactions.

Now, Allie was also a very attractive child, but she's a blonde. And in Minnesota, blonds are as common as frostbite and mosquitoes.

Fortunately, within a couple days of Anji's arrival, Allie was simply enthralled with her little sister, "my very own live baby." The jealousy was over and they became inseparable. In Allie's kindergarten class, each week a different student would take home the "Show-and-Tell Bucket," a heart-shaped bright red plastic pail about sixteen inches in diameter and perhaps fourteen inches high. The next day the child would return with something in the bucket that was interesting to share. For Allie's turn, when it came time for show-and-tell, she went out into the hallway and returned with her little sister in the bucket. That was a hit.

To this day, though they are quite different in many ways, Allie and Anji remain great friends, even to the point that when the girls stay over at our house, they choose to share a bed.

Jay Serafino reports:

> Katrin Schumann, co-author of *The Secret Power of Middle Children*, has done extensive research on the subject that found the plight of middle children may actually be a positive thing later in life. One such trait is their ability to negotiate.
>
> "Middles are used to not getting their own way, and so they become savvy, skillful manipulators," Schumann told *Psychology Today*. "They can see all sides of a question and are empathetic and judge reactions well. They are more willing to compromise, and so they can argue successfully. Since they often have to wait around as kids, they're more patient."

I hadn't thought about this before as a product of my birth order, but my mother often commented about how easy I was as a kid. "I could take you anywhere and simply plop you down in the corner with your plastic farm animals and you'd play by yourself for hours." I really was patient. Especially compared to our children. Allie somehow missed that memo.

That same article notes the following:

> Though the conventional numbers have established that most U.S. presidents are firstborns, Schumann contends that

half of our Commanders-in-Chief are actually middle children. In an interview with NPR, she revealed that the connection between the presidency and middle children was obscured for years because of one strange quirk: firstborn girls weren't traditionally counted as older siblings.

Good grief.

One place Allie certainly did not exhibit the typical middle child's ability to negotiate and be patient was on the basketball floor, where she was often the smallest girl on the court. For years she played point guard and played it with gusto and scrappiness. In the years I coached, she fouled out more than all of the other players combined. During one game, the referee actually stopped the action and came over to talk to me: "Coach, you have to get that number 5 to calm down. She's too aggressive. She's going to hurt somebody."

Today, Allie is well adjusted, with lots of good friendships. She is a consistent high achiever, a recent graduate from a prestigious law school.

Not bad for a middle child.

Would We Do It Again?

R ight now, you have times in which you are happy and times in which you are unhappy," said my cousin. At the happy part, he held his left hand eye high, palm down; and at the sad part, he moved his right hand down to waist high, palm up. His hands were now a couple feet apart. Terry was four years older than I and married with two little kids. I was a few weeks away from my wedding. The extended family was celebrating a cousin's birthday in the living room of Terry's parents' home. He was giving me this advice based on personal experience from the past few years.

"Then, when you get married, sometimes you are happy . . ." (left hand held several inches above his head) ". . . and other times you are unhappy" (right hand now several inches below his waist). "And then when you have kids, you are sometimes happy . . ." (left hand as high up as he could reach) ". . . and sometimes you are unhappy" (right hand as low as he could reach). He concluded: "You simply cannot imagine right now the extremes of emotions that await you."

I've thought of Terry's analysis and warning dozens of times since—usually during the hardest moments of marriage or parenting. He could not have been more right.

Let's consider the joys and pains of parenting.

We have a twenty-nine-year-old relative who recently stated he couldn't imagine ever having children. He has bipolar disorder but is dealing with it quite successfully. Relaying his statement, I remarked to my spouse, "That's probably a good choice for him. Having kids will cause the most modulated human being to become bipolar."

My wife chuckled . . . and then went off for a good cry.

Our kids are all in their twenties now, perhaps the most challenging time for parents, at least those parents whose kids didn't go off the rails in the teenage years. Everyone knows the old saying "Little kids, little problems. Big kids, big problems." Obviously, little ones require every-second vigilance on the part of parents. But the trouble little kids can get into is rather limited, provided parents childproof their house and keep the young'uns out of the street. However, the amount of trouble semigrown kids, sometimes known as *young adults*, can get into is virtually limitless. And one bad decision can quickly lead to . . . well, death . . . or worse.

When we moved into our house, our older kids were five and three. The littlest one had not yet joined the family. The next-door neighbor's kids were now grown. One day, she told me how hard it was that her husband worked nights. She noted that when her teenagers got in trouble (usually at night, of course), Dad was off at work. "It was hard, you know . . . When the police would come—"

"When the *police* would come?" I thought to myself, shocked, utterly unable to imagine my little cherubs in any situation that would call for police interaction.

Fifteen years later, I had a couple of opportunities to realize I may have been a bit hasty in judging my neighbor's kids.

Okay, I'll admit it. When I was eighteen, I had my own encounter with jail, but I had the good sense—okay, good luck—not to let my parents know about it. (By the way, my partner in crime and fellow arrestee also eventually turned out to be a Presbyterian pastor. Life is funny, isn't it?)

To save my kids further embarrassment, I will spare you the details of their adventures over the past few years. But as we talk with so many other parents facing similar issues, we've also discovered ours are not out-of-the-ordinary challenges.

For the past few years, I keep having the same dream over and over. I'm supposed to be driving a bus, but the trouble is I'm not in the driver's seat. I'm back a seat or two. The bus is heading down the road at sixty miles per hour and no one is driving! I'm supposed to be, but I can't reach the steering wheel or the brakes. I frantically try to claw my way to the front as the bus careens off the road. Then I wake up, heart pounding, sleep ended for the night.

It doesn't take Freud to figure this one out. I'm having trouble letting go of the wheel of my kids' lives. I have so much hard-earned wisdom that is going to waste here as my kids fail to ask for my excellent advice. Just yesterday I saw this sign: "Dad's always right—but no one listens."

Years ago I heard a famous psychiatrist say, "I've been a therapist for thirty years and seen thousands of clients. Each of my clients has the exact same problem—the people in their lives won't do what they want them to do." I think of that saying at least three times a week: my kids often don't do what I want them to do; my spouse occasionally doesn't do what I want her to do; my parishioners sometimes don't do what I want them to do; the president doesn't do what I want him to do; even *I* don't do what I want me to do. (See Romans 7 on that last one.)

Control. That subject is worth an essay of its own.

I am happy to report the kids seem to have matured out of the crisis stage—cerebral cortexes finally fully formed—and I seem to be maturing in my ability to let go.

We've all heard that old chestnut: "Let go . . . and let God." Easy to say; hard to do. Lately I heard a pithier version, one with powerful motivation behind it: "Let go . . . or be dragged."

Parenting was so fun when the kids were young. Little kids have been compared to pet dogs. They are eager to please and are hungry for affection. But as they enter into the teen years, they morph into cats—eager to be independent and disdainful of all attempts to interact.

Many people of a certain age will remember that the advice columnist Ann Landers once asked her readers, "If you had it to do over again, would you have children?" A few weeks later her column was headlined "70 Percent of Parents Say Kids Not Worth It." Indeed, 70 percent of the nearly 10,000 parents who wrote in said they would not have children if they could make the choice again. I'm guessing these were mostly parents of fifteen- to-twenty-five-year-olds.

Of course, those readers are the ones who took the trouble to write in. A poll of random parents taken by *Newsday* two months later found 91 percent of parents *would* have children again. Certainly my wife and I are in that 91 percent. Most of the time. And I try not to think about the fact the typical American child costs its parents a reported two or three hundred thousand dollars.

We do love our children beyond anything we could have ever imagined. And they have provided us with memories both precious and comical. As our kids were growing up, my spouse and I kept a journal for each of the three kids, trying to capture the memorable, and often hilarious, things they did and said. Reading through the books now as a family is a great joy. What did we laugh at before we had kids?

This is from the journal we kept about our eldest, Andy: One day he observed, "I used to want to play basketball in order to get girls when I was little. But now I find that I like the game." (He was eight years old when he said this.)

Andy and I were driving in the car one day, just the two of us. He was now nine years old and absolutely bonkers over basketball, soccer, and baseball, utterly convinced he was going to play in the NBA one day. Given his genes (I couldn't make my high school team), I thought it might be good for him to have a plan B. I asked, "What do you want to be when you grow up?"

"A professional basketball or baseball player."

"What if you can't be an athlete?"

"A coach."

"Ah, what would you choose to be if it weren't in sports?"

"Does an umpire or referee count?"

"Yes."

"A scorekeeper?"

"Are you serious, or are you just trying to bug me?" I really couldn't tell if Andy was just yanking my chain. Could he really think of no possible vocation outside of sports?

A few seconds of pondering . . . "Well, if I couldn't be in sports, I guess maybe I'll be a terminator."

Confused, and thinking about the movie, I asked, "What's that?"

"You know, when you kill the bugs in people's houses."

When Andy was twelve, his mother asked if he'd ever kissed anyone. "No, but it's not that I couldn't have, if I had wanted to."

That's my boy.

And then Allie, next in line. At four, she spouted questions faster than we could answer them: "Can squirrels read?" "Do ducks have ears?"

And she was always hungry. At six she said, "Remember, I'm in a girl sprouts."

"What?"

Oh, a *growth spurt.*

When she was about that same age, I went Rollerblading with her one afternoon. After a couple of falls she noted, "Next time I'm wearing my helmet on my butt."

Allie, at age twelve: "I just had the biggest dump! Weighed myself; lost two pounds!"

At sixteen, as she came into the kitchen one morning, her mother hugged her and said, "Mmmmmm, you smell nice."

"I just pooped."

I know you are thinking she will be mortified to see these anecdotes in print, but trust me, it won't bother her a bit. She's proudly earthy.

When Anji was ten, she and I were taking a walk together one evening. She eagerly told about her day. Then she asked, "How was your day?"

I started to tell her, and then she remembered something else about her day and interrupted to tell me.

I said, "Honey, when you ask how someone's day is, you should really listen."

"I know, but it's hard."

"It is hard, but you like it when people really listen to you."

"I don't really care if people listen. I just love to talk."

Finally, we have this, from when she was five: It was Christmas morning, about ten o'clock, and the family was done opening presents. Anji observed, "The gifts aren't my Christmas present. Being with my family is my Christmas present."

Cousin Terry was so right—the lows are low, but the highs are so high.

ON

Being

FAITHFUL

ON HUMILITY

Now, what I am about to tell you is true. I know you won't believe it. I certainly wouldn't if I read it in a book. So I won't be surprised or offended if you don't believe me.

But it *is* true. Factual. Happened. I have 200 witnesses.

I stepped into the pulpit on a warm and humid June morning. Outside, a few clouds were gathering. The congregation looked up at me in eager anticipation (I was still pretty new among them). I announced, "Today I'm going to preach on the subject of humility. And before I begin, I want you to know I worked especially hard on my sermon this week. I put a *lot* of time into it. And I think I was unusually inspired. I feel really good about this. In fact, my friends, this may just be the *best* sermon on humility ever preached."

One second after my little joke—one!—a tremendous bolt of lightning flashed. Simultaneously, the loudest crash of thunder I think any of us had ever heard exploded around us. Ginormous! It continued to rumble and grumble for at least ten seconds. After a few moments of utterly stunned silence, we all began to roar with laughter. I was laughing so hard myself I wasn't sure I could preach. I thought I might have to sit down for a while to gather myself.

Finally, I looked heavenward. Then I managed to squeak out, "Okay, maybe the *second* best . . ."

On Reading

We like to encourage children to be in worship, if possible. For the younger ones, we have a play area up front with various toys. We also have "busy bags" for use in the pews. These contain markers and coloring books, small plush toys, Bible stories, and other creative things. Our children's ministry puts them together each week. We like for kids to experience and learn about worship, at least by osmosis, and to know they are welcome in all facets of church life.

A lot of the older kids simply bring a book to read during the service. Mollie was one such child: an eight-year-old who loved to read, perfectly content to get lost in a book while worship went on around her. A lovelier and sweeter child I've never met.

One memorable Sunday, Mollie and her family were seated in the front row of the transept, just about a dozen feet from the pulpit. As usual, Mollie was engrossed in her book. Then at one point she paused, put a finger in the pages to hold her place, and spoke to her mother. Her loud stage whisper was heard throughout the congregation.

"Mom, what's a wet dream?"

The 3 Percent

"A hot day and a stubborn mule have called many a man into the ministry." (As the word *mule* would indicate, this saying comes from a long time ago, a time when women may have been "called" into ministry but certainly weren't allowed to pursue that call.)

As someone who grew up on a farm, I often reflect with gratitude on the fact I have an "indoor job." We didn't have any mules to deal with when I was a child, but picking sweet corn on a hot and humid day is no Sunday School picnic. Cornstalk leaves are switchblade sharp, so the corn picker, even on the hottest days, has to wear long pants and a sturdy long-sleeve shirt. To free both of your hands for picking, you attach the gunnysack in front of you on two curved hooks protruding from your "corn belt," and as that sack fills, it gets heavy. When it starts dragging on the ground between your legs, you get back-bent and bowlegged. Five dozen ears makes for some slow slogging, let me tell you. And on muddy days, when the pickup can't drive down the row, you're slinging two or three bags at a time onto your back, then trudging through the muck to the end of the row where the truck awaits. Throw in the mosquitoes and horse-flies, and, yes, the pastorate seems like a mighty cushy alternative.

And yet there are some days when I could be tempted to trade what I do for farmwork, even at its worst.

Now, there are not *many* of these days. I often say, "Ninety percent of my job as a pastor I would do for free. Seven percent I could take or leave. And that last three percent? Well, there really isn't enough money in the world . . . It's a calling."

A friend of mine once confessed that, until knowing me, he thought a pastor lived a largely contemplative life of books and prayer. Ohhh, that sounds heavenly.

It does *not* describe the life of a modern pastor, however. Most pastors would readily acknowledge there *should* be more prayer and reading in our lives, but the demands of the modern parish complicate life significantly.

My experience as a pastor has, for the most part—that "90 percent" part—been extremely rewarding. What a deep and holy privilege it is to be with people at the most meaningful times of their lives—birth, marriage, illness, death. I love interacting with people of all ages—from receiving sticky high fives and refrigerator art from the toddlers to hearing the stories of nonagenarians who have lived through the Great Depression and World War II. And even after forty years of ministry, I frequently marvel over how lucky I am to get paid to study the Bible . . . and to wrestle with important subjects like grace and faith and the meaning of life.

Some parts of a pastor's job are less fun. That 7 percent which I "could take or leave" is made up of facing the dozens of daily emails awaiting me anew every morning, as well as supervising the staff, balancing the budget, and attending committee meetings. In my career, I have participated in approximately three thousand committee meetings. They hold less interest for me now than when I was still in my first thousand.

And what about that final yucky 3 percent? That consists of dealing with unhappy parishioners.

Sometimes people have utterly legitimate complaints. When I think back on some of the mistakes I made as a young pastor, I simply cringe and thank God for that first congregation I served. Such gracious and forgiving folks!

And I am not done making mistakes, by any means.

But it seems to me that some people who are simply unhappy in life, and who don't have any power elsewhere in their lives, take it out on the church. (For more on this subject, see the final essay: "To Know the Whole Story.") And, of course, as the Church faithfully does its job of being the Church—welcoming and comforting the afflicted, the hurting, and the unwell—we encounter a lot of, shall we say, "interesting" people.

In the last generation, we have seen hundreds of second-career pastors, folks who, after years of taking immense enjoyment in being active members of their home congregations, feel called into ordained ministry. They go to seminary and then enter into pastoral ministry with high hopes and unbridled enthusiasm. A fairly high percentage of them scurry back to their former calling after one brief pastorate. They discover things can look a little different from the inside.

In the most challenging congregation I have served was a lovely old guy who had been the town shoe repairman for four decades. Now he was retired, and he spent his time tending his flowers along the riverbank at the back of his lot. He was a small man with a sweet smile and a gentle spirit. After reading about the stresses of the pastorate, he from time to time would check in on me. "Bill, are *you* stressed? Don't let us stress you," he would say with a compassionate look of concern and a slight shake of his head.

I would reply, "Thanks, Stan. I really appreciate that." And I did. But at the same time, I was thinking, "You know what, Stan? If you would just drown your next-door neighbor, I wouldn't feel stressed at all."

One of my heroes in ministry told me a story about a particular Sunday, one of those magical mornings in which everything came together. The little kids performing in an all-age program had done so with amazing professionalism and unbearable cuteness; the adult choir had been marvelous, the sopranos hitting those impossibly high notes and sending chills down everyone's spines; and the youth had been equally amazing, sharing their surprisingly profound insights on faith and life. Everyone was celebrating what a grand morning it had been.

Well, not everyone.

My friend was putting his robe away, his heart filled with joy at the privilege of being a minister. Then he heard a voice. It called, "Reverend . . ."

Immediately, his body tensed. He knew that voice. It was that one parishioner who could *always* find something to complain about; and indeed, even on this glorious morning, she had found it. One tiny little thing that wasn't perfect . . . and she proceeded to gripe and whine about it.

He took a deep breath. Let it out. And then let out something else—the frustrations of fifteen years of parish ministry and this woman's constant string of grievances. He looked her in the eye and said, quietly and evenly, smiling slightly, "You really are a bitch, aren't you?"

You can see why he's one of my heroes.

Another pastor friend of mine famously named his ulcers after church members. "This one—" (pointing to his side) "—is Mrs. Johnson. Over here we have Fred Schwartz," and so on.

And at times things get really serious. One of my pastor friends ticked off someone to the point he actually received a death threat from a disgruntled parishioner. My friend contacted the police, who took the warning very seriously. They loaned him a bullet-proof vest to wear under his robe and stationed a sharpshooter in the balcony for ten consecutive Sundays.

And just what was the issue that set this person off. Abortion? Homosexuality? The firing of a beloved staff person?

No—bulletin covers.

Seriously. Bulletin covers.

Every congregation has some slightly, shall we say, "off-kilter" members. In my capacity as a pastor, I have felt my life was in actual danger from disturbed individuals no fewer than four times.

Yes, there are some days when I miss working on the farm . . .

My farmer dad was the only person I ever met who actually liked to hoe, the single most boring activity I have ever encountered—though you can't argue with his reason for enjoying it.

"Nobody's bothering you," he would say.

Now, before I share one more story, I want to repeat that in my experience, the rewards of parish ministry vastly outweigh the challenges. Remember where I started. How many people do you know who can say "Ninety percent of my job I would do for free"? I hope the rest of this book accurately reflects this sentiment.

But here's my favorite. A friend once told me the story of her brother, who spent a few years as a Lutheran pastor until, after one too many ulcer-inducing parishioners, he felt the Lord's call to become a plumber. According to the sister, one day he had just finished installing all the new plumbing in a house. Down in the basement, showing the homeowner what he had done, he said, "Well, let's see if it works" and turned a valve.

The swish of liquid could be heard racing through the pipes. Then there was a groaning noise. The pipes started to shake violently. Finally, *kablooey*! Pipes burst and their contents sprayed all over the basement. By the time the valve was shut off, the plumber and homeowner were covered nose-to-toes in human waste.

Coughing and sputtering, they wiped themselves off. Eventually, the homeowner turned to the plumber and said, "Well, I bet this makes you wish you were back in the pulpit."

The plumber considered this for a moment. Then he said cheerily, "Oh, no. *This* shit I can wash off."

ON FUN

The helicopter buzzed past my face, not five feet in front of me.

A few years back I was walking with my family through a shopping mall, on our way to a restaurant, when we came across a kiosk selling toy helicopters you can fly with a remote control. The salesperson made a copter go up, turn left and right, zip forward, *zip backward*, and gently descend for a perfect landing. I had not seen these toys before, nor had I even heard of such a thing. (Of course, my children had.) I was mesmerized.

"How cool is that?" I said.

We proceeded on to dinner, and I didn't give toy helicopters another thought until a few weeks later, on Christmas morning. I opened my present from my twenty-three-year-old son: my very own remote-control helicopter! About twelve inches long, black with silver markings. And a headlight that actually worked. I was utterly surprised and absolutely delighted, both with the present and with my son's thoughtfulness.

I loved the helicopter! I still love it.

Not long after, I used it in a children's sermon one Sunday. The chopper took off from the communion table, flew thirty feet up in the air, veered left, and swooped down toward the organist. I flew it back up, sent it to the rear of the sanctuary, then took it on its final loop back to the communion table, where I gave it a (fairly) gentle landing. The kids—and the adults—watched with open mouths and laughing faces. As the chopper landed, they exclaimed and cheered!

I explained to the kids the point of this display: to illustrate the joy my son experienced in giving me this present and seeing the delight on my face. How fun it is to give! Though I don't know that we actually *needed* a "point" beyond "Look at this cool thing!" Everyone was enchanted, especially the ninety-year-olds. After the service, more than one person commented at the door, "Well, I never expected to see the minister flying a helicopter in church . . ." before adding, "But was that ever *cool*!" (Okay, the ninety-year-olds didn't use the word *cool*. But believe me, they loved it.)

I keep the helicopter on top of a filing cabinet in my office; it charges up from my computer. Once in a while, I'll take a break from work, grab the chopper, and fly it around the church.

Recently, a longtime friend of the church stopped by my office. Dave used to live in the apartments across the street. Occasionally, we had helped him out with a grocery card or a phone bill and, in return, he sometimes did a little painting around the church. Then he moved twenty miles away and we lost touch. Now here he was again. In the eighteen months since I had last seen him, his hair had gone entirely white, he had lost ten pounds off his already skinny-as-a-scarecrow frame, and the expression on his face had become exceedingly dour—one would think he had just run over his dog.

In the past, he had usually been animated and reasonably upbeat about the future. But now, as he caught me up on recent history, Dave alternated between slumping in a chair muttering softly, and jumping up to pace the floor of my office. His hands twitched and clenched. Turns out he had lost his apartment some months back and had been living out of his car. But now his car had died. And winter was coming.

"I can't take another winter outside," he said. "And every single time I been to a shelter, I got robbed! I just don't know what to do, Bill. I got nothing! I don't know if it's worth going on."

I had seen him low on occasion, but not like this.

We talked about some housing options. I gave him a grocery card and a few dollars to tide him over until he received his next disability check. He nodded and thanked me but continued pacing my office.

And then he spotted it: "A helicopter! This yours?"

I explained how I had become the proud owner of this chopper.

"It really flies?" Dave asked.

"Certainly. Watch." And with that we headed to the sanctuary. I set the toy on the communion table and slowly lifted it off. Dave cackled, "Huh! Lookee there! Oh, my *goodness!*" He clasped his hands, gazing with pure excitement as the chopper ascended, nearly touched the ceiling, then zoomed thirty feet away and turned 180 degrees. I buzzed it past his ear. Dave hooted and hollered!

I landed the copter on the communion table and handed him the controls. "Your turn."

"Oh, I don't know . . ." Dave shook his head. "I don't want to wreck it."

"It's pretty durable," I said. "I've crashed it a bunch of times."

I explained how the controls worked. Soon Dave was flying it around the sanctuary, grinning like he had won the lottery.

When we had finished, he said, "That was just what the doctor ordered, Bill. I was so low, but flying that helicopter . . . Man, that was something! Thank you. You have cheered me *up!*"

The psychologist Abraham Maslow talked about the hierarchy of needs—things like food, shelter, and safety forming the foundation levels. But Dave showed me the power of—and need for—fun, even when some of the basics are temporarily missing.

The Christian activist and editor of *Sojourners* magazine, Jim Wallis, tells a story from the civil wars in Central America in the 1980s. A young woman from the US was volunteering in one of the refugee camps. Refugee camps are heartbreaking by definition. But this was a particularly dire situation. From time to time, this young woman would swim across the nearby river in the dark of night, to return with a child on her back. She'd bring the little one to safety, never knowing when the helicopter gunships would arrive to spray the water.

On a typical day, she worked from before dawn until she dropped onto her cot long after dark.

One Saturday night, the refugee camp had a party. That's right—a party. The refugees had formed three committees for the overall welfare of the camp—a Health Committee, an Education Committee, and a Committee for Fun! This last committee had organized the party. But the young volunteer did not want to go. She stayed back and kept working despite repeated cajoling from the folks in the camp.

"I have work to do," she said. "I don't have time to party."

An old woman from the camp walked up to the young woman and pointed a crooked finger in her face. "That's right. You can keep on working. Because in a few months, you will go home. But we will still be here. That's why we need to party."

The volunteer went to celebrate with everyone else. And, of course, it was just what she needed too.

We Presbyterians have gotten a bad rap over the years. Granted, often a well-deserved bad rap. No essay on "fun" could leave off the famous passage from John Steinbeck's *East of Eden* that my

Lutheran friends like to tease me with (yes, those wild and crazy Lutherans!):

> He brought with him his tiny Irish wife, a tight hard little woman humor-less as a chicken. She had a dour Presbyterian mind and a code of morals that pinned down and beat the brains out of nearly everything that was pleasant to do.

What? For Presbyterians, *fun* is the f-word?

Recently I was asked to say grace at a reception following a wedding I had just officiated. After getting the crowd to be quiet, I said, "Jesus loved a party. Remember that Jesus' critics called him 'a glutton and a drunkard.'* So it is with joy and the blessing of Jesus that we come to this feast." Then I offered a prayer of thanks.

As soon as the prayer was over, one of the young groomsmen came up to me with an incredulous look. "Jesus was called 'a glutton and a drunkard'?" he said. "Really?"

I nodded.

"Wow! I never knew that!" And the young man's obvious newfound appreciation for Jesus brought both of us, I think, great pleasure and delight.

---

* It's Matthew 11:19 and Luke 7:34, if you don't believe me.

THE PRESENCE

In his day, Dad was a large and powerful man, able to yank three gunnysacks of sweet corn at a time off the ground, then swing them around onto his back. He carried the sacks—sixty-five ears in each—a hundred yards to the waiting truck, the muddy ground threatening to suck his boots right off his feet with every step.

But by his sixties, eroding hip sockets had slowed Dad down considerably. For whatever reason, he put surgery off for years. Finally, he had his right hip replaced. The operation went well; recovery was quick and he was soon back on the farm, albeit still limping because of the left hip.

A year later, he went in for surgery to replace that joint. Based on his first surgery, we expected Dad to breeze through this one as well. I saw him right after the operation, and things looked to be going fine.

A few days passed. Then early one afternoon, I was in my church study working on my sermon when I got a phone call from my older brother, Cal.

"Dad's not recovering as well this time around," he said.

"Really?" I said. "He seemed pretty good when I saw him."

"He's in a lot of pain," said Cal. "If you have time, could you go see him, please?"

I hadn't been there for a few days. I knew my siblings, who all lived closer to my parents than I did, had been checking in on him regularly. And, of course, he'd already been through one of these operations. I said of course and asked if I should come right away.

"No, no giant hurry," Cal said. "When it's convenient."

I told him I would come the following evening and we hung up. But when I tried to get back to my sermon, I found I couldn't concentrate.

"I think I'll go now," I said to myself. "Why not, if it would make me feel better?" But still I wasn't really that concerned; Cal had said it wasn't urgent.

I felt differently as soon as I turned into Dad's hospital room. His face was gray and racked with pain, and my mother, sitting next to him holding his hand, was visibly distraught. My insides turned to stone. I couldn't breathe.

I had done a fair amount of hospital calling by then, and I processed immediately what I was walking into: I knew what people looked like when they were getting better, and I knew what people looked like when they weren't.

As a pastor, I was used to parishioners dying. But these were my parents. The fear that was already filling the room intensified as I stepped in and added my own. This was an entirely different experience.

After just a few moments of terror-stricken small talk, I suggested, "How about if we pray?" Now, other than grace at meals, we had never done a lot of—any?—praying together as a family. But both of my parents nodded eagerly. So I stood on one side of the bed, Mom sat on the other, and the three of us held hands and shut our eyes. I took a deep breath and then prayed something like this: "Dear Jesus"—in seminary we were taught to pray to God, not Jesus, but when I'm in trouble, I go straight to my main man—"Dear Jesus, you made the deaf to hear, the blind to see, the lame to walk . . . Please heal Dad . . ."

And into that hospital room came a palpable presence of peace. Jesus was there. It was *exactly* as if there were four of us now, holding hands. I actually peeked to see if that were literally true. It wasn't, but Jesus was there.

I took a deep breath and fully opened my eyes. The lines of pain had dissolved from Dad's face and some color had returned to it. The hopelessness on Mom's face had been replaced with an expression of calm, of trust.

From that moment, Dad started getting better.

But that's not the point of this story. Dad died of something else a few years later. The point is this: it no longer mattered if Dad got better or not.

Because Jesus was there.

Now, I don't have a lot of "spiritual experiences" like this one. Perhaps because I am not aware enough to notice them. And certainly there are other ways to interpret what happened. Perhaps Dad would have recovered without that prayer. But for me, this was truly a miracle, by the definition I memorized forty years ago and still know word for word. That early-twentieth-century pulpit giant George Buttrick wrote: "A miracle is any event so ordered as to break through our dullness or despair to convince us of the presence of God."

In that hospital room something broke through our despair, our fear.

I believe it was Jesus.

ON ANGER

The other day, I did something I have never done before. And I am now at an age where that doesn't happen very often.

It was an ordinary trip to the local hardware store. As I approached the store, I slowed and signaled to make a right turn into the parking lot. But a couple of boys, about twelve years old, were walking up the sidewalk toward the driveway. So, with a glance in my rearview mirror, I came to a stop in the right lane of traffic and waved the boys across. The car behind me stopped, but when the boys were halfway across the driveway, this driver let out an angry blast on his horn.

Huh? Man, that steamed my mussels. My turn signal was on. The driver behind me could certainly see the boys in my way. "Seriously? You want me to run them over?"

In hindsight, I kind of wished I had calmly put my car in park—right there in the lane of traffic—turned on my flashers, stepped out of my car, walked back to the driver behind me, and calmly asked him that question: "You want me to run them over?"

But I didn't.

This is what I did. After the boys had crossed the driveway, and as I started my right turn and the driver went by me on the left, I stuck my arm out the window and gave him a one-finger salute.

First time in my life. Really. And I am well past the half-century mark, when I should be getting calmer . . . and wiser . . . and more mature.

I'll admit it wasn't one of my finest moments.

Now, it is certainly okay to get mad. Anger is a normal human emotion, and I contend that, like all other emotions, such as joy and peacefulness—even fear and sadness—anger is a gift from God.

The trick is to harness it and to use it appropriately.

In the Beatitudes (Matthew 5), the very core of Jesus' teaching, he says, "Blessed are the meek, for they shall inherit the earth."

In this era of assertiveness training and "looking out for number one," the idea of cultivating meekness might seem absurd. In fact, *meek* does not seem to be a popular word these days; when was the last time you heard it in a conversation? But what we think of when we hear the word *meek*—an attitude of subservience, of self-negation, of *cowardice*, even—is *not* what Jesus was talking about. For certainly Jesus himself was none of those things.

We think of meekness as never getting angry. But Jesus showed righteous anger when he threw the money changers out of the temple; when his disciples tried to keep children from bothering him; when he countered the scribes and Pharisees—calling a Jew a "whitewashed tomb" (Matthew 23:27), which would be the insult equivalent of "F—— you" today—and perhaps even when he rebuked Simon Peter: "Get behind me, Satan!"

The New Testament Greek word translated in some versions as *meek* in Jesus' "Blessed are the meek" line is *praus*. The same word, *praus,* is used in Matthew 21:5 to describe Jesus just before he wreaks havoc in the temple. And one of the descriptions of someone who is *praus* is this: "a person who is never angry at the wrong time but always angry at the right time."

Now, that is something to which we might all aspire.

In all those examples I gave from Jesus' life, his anger was directed at protecting other people, not himself. As the author of 1 Peter (2:23) notes about Jesus, "when he was reviled, did not revile in return, when he suffered, he did not threaten . . ." In the Garden of Gethsemane when Peter tried to defend Jesus by pulling out a sword, Jesus said, "Oh, for Pete's sake! Don't you know I could call down twelve legions of angels to fight for me?"

Instead of expending fury at the person who honks at us, or who cuts us off in traffic, or who has more than ten items in the express lane (my personal hot button), we might direct that anger toward issues of true importance—children not having enough to eat; corporations polluting the air and water; politicians habitually lying; people of color, or members of the LGBTQ+ community, or females, or immigrants being treated as "less than." *That's* the time for anger. That's the time for true "meekness."

No more one-finger salutes. That just throws gas on the fire. I failed to consider what kind of day this driver might have been having before his stupid honk. I didn't know the whole story. But more than that, it just wasn't important. My anger was about me, not about some form of injustice.

"Blessed are those who are never angry at the wrong time, but always angry at the right time," said Jesus.

ON BEING A "CHRISTIAN"

*I'd rather face 10,000 devils from hell than one Christian
convinced that he's right.*

—*Anonymous*

It has been well noted that in the last generation, the fundamentalist wing of the Christian Church made an intentional move that has had a monumental impact on politics, culture, and religion itself. Fundamentalists used to try to avoid attention in the public square; now they seek it out. They've been so successful in doing so that, today, they almost completely dominate media coverage of the Church.

And what is it fundamentalists are asserting so loudly in the name of Christ? Many of the self-proclaimed "Christians" on television and radio have in recent years promoted a violent, xenophobic, and misogynistic platform. Their shouted tirades and rants are racist, pro–military action, homophobic, anti-immigrant, anti-conservation, anti-gun control laws, anti-women . . . the list goes on and on and on.

I find this simply astonishing. In my opinion, these people are clearly reading a different Bible than I am. And so many of them are personally mean-spirited as they spew their vitriol: the Reverend Jerry Falwell once called NOW (the National Organization of Women) the "National Order of Witches." On a regular basis, far-right media pundit Ann Coulter throws out every vulgar and hateful playground insult she can think of at political and cultural figures. Her language is so ugly; I can't even get myself to quote it here. What a horrible witness to Jesus!

I could write many pages on the issues I listed above, explaining exactly what I believe Jesus teaches about each of them; it is probably already clear I believe those teachings contradict what so many of these television personalities espouse by 180 degrees.

But that has been done. I have a more personal point to make.

By dominating the airwaves, these spokespeople for the so-called Christian Right have absolutely polluted that sacred word. I find it embarrassing these days to identify myself as a "Christian." When my twenty-something-year-old children are asked by a new acquaintance what their father does for a living, they have to immediately follow "He's a pastor" with a hurried explanation: "But not *that* kind of a pastor. He's very progressive, not antigay or anything. He's one of the good ones."

The congregation I am privileged to experience on a daily basis is a hospitable community of inclusion. It cares for the poor and oppressed and works to protect the earth. But what nonbelievers see and hear on television is a self-proclaimed "Church" that is none of those things. No wonder fewer and fewer people take the Church seriously. Recent polls show Americans turning away from religion in larger numbers than ever. Who can blame them, when they imagine they'll be going to church with these viperish haters?

The actor/comedian John Fugelsang has said, "For me, Jesus is like Elvis. Love the man; the fan club freaks me out."

What a fantastic line! Not to *equate* Jesus with Elvis, for heaven's sake (literally!), but Fugelsang makes a superb point about so much of the Church today. "Those" people freak me out too!

I no longer even use the term *Christian* to describe my faith stance (hence my careful use of quotation marks).

Instead I say, "I try to follow Jesus."

Another wonderful quote from Fugelsang:

> Jesus was a radical nonviolent revolutionary who hung around with lepers, hookers, and crooks; wasn't American and never spoke English; was anti-wealth, anti-death penalty, anti-public prayer (Matt. 6:5); but was never anti-gay, never mentioned abortion or birth control, never called the poor lazy, never justified torture, never fought for tax cuts for the wealthiest Nazarenes, never asked a leper for a copay; and was a long-haired brown-skinned homeless community-organizing anti-slut-shaming Middle Eastern Jew.

ON PROGNOSTICATION

No one can predict the future."

We hear that statement all the time, and most accept it as a truism. Yet we can and do predict the future every day. In fact, in certain situations our very survival depends on our ability to predict the future.

No doubt our ancestors learned to predict that if they bothered that den of saber-toothed tigers, then they—our ancestors—wouldn't have to grumble about the long walk to the creek anymore. We can predict that if we step in front of a speeding train, then our afternoon will be ruined. We can predict that if we make that sarcastic comment about our boss—in her earshot—we'll have time to go fishing next week.

Of course, those are all obvious things. Here are three real-life prognostications from my own life.

1. A few decades ago, I got inside info on a small company that was pioneering in the field of computer programs for farmers. Computers were certainly the wave of the future. This seemed like a can't-miss proposition. I eagerly invested $2,500—a lot of money for a small-town pastor in 1982—while visions of IBM danced in my head.

2. The Jorgensons (not their real name, to protect the guilty) were the first family in the congregation to invite me over for dinner after I began service as the pastor of their church. We discovered we had a lot in common. Really nice folks. As I drove home at the end of a lovely evening, I thought, "I'll bet they become some of my very best friends."

3. A few years into our marriage, my wife said to me one evening, "Remember Shari?"

"Sure," I said. Shari was a friend of hers from college.

"She's expanding her futon-cover business. You know, they're doing really well. She and her sister started in their basement, and now they're in the garage."

"Is that considered a move up?" I asked.

My wife gave me a look and went on. "She'd like to rent a building and hire some employees, and she's looking for investors. Whaddya think about putting a few thousand dollars in? If things go well, we could make a lot of money."

"What do I think?" Immediately, I came up with several objections.

One: Futon covers. A fad that would surely fade, like pet rocks and Chia Pets.

Two: I didn't know Shari very well. But I did know she had been an *art major,* for heaven's sake. What did she know about business?

Three: "A few thousand dollars" was the sum total of our cash on hand.

But I didn't voice any of this out loud. Instead I said, "Gosh ... that's interesting. But it's just that, if things *don't* go well, we're out the money *and* it puts a strain on your friendship. I really don't think it's a good idea."

My spouse acquiesced. We did not invest.

Jump ahead to the future.

1. Within a few years that stock in agricultural computer services, which cost me only $2,500, had mushroomed to a total value of $625.

2. The Jorgensons, a year or so after our lovely evening, led a small group of congregation members that tried to fire me.

3. The futon company? A few years, two factories, and 120 employees later, Shari turned down an offer to sell the company for five million dollars.

My crystal ball seems to be a bit cloudy. I have seriously thought about starting my own stock market newsletter, offering what seem to me to be logical tips but warning my readers always to do . . . the opposite.

I do take comfort in a couple examples of faulty predictions by others. Many of us know about that high school basketball coach who cut from the squad a youngster by the name of Michael Jordan. Lesser known is the prognostication of Lt. Joseph Christmas Ives, who wins top honors in the history of American travel writing for his classic misjudgment of interest in a certain travel destination. After leading an expedition through the American Southwest in 1857 and viewing the Grand Canyon, he wrote, "Ours has been the first, and will doubtless be the last, party of whites to visit this profitless locality."

Faulty predictions can cost us money, and they can cost us our lives (saber-toothed tigers, speeding trains). But, if we survive our faulty predictions, they can also *give* us some things: humility, obviously, and a sense of irony (both qualities glaringly absent in many of today's business and political leaders).

But above all, acknowledging we've made a few major-league boneheaded predictions can also give us a certain sense of adventure about life. We love to be in control. (At least we can see *other* people have "control issues.") However, if we can acknowledge that not only do we not *control* much of life, we can't even *guess* what it's going to be like, then perhaps we can relax a bit and enjoy being surprised—at times amazed—at what life serves up.

I offer one more example of my scintillating ability to discern the future.

"Hey, Bill, I have a favor to ask . . . There's a young filmmaker in the area working on a science-fiction flick, and he's got a couple guys here who would like to use the chapel to record some sound effects. If that's okay, would you mind unlocking the door for us?"

The questioner was my fellow seminarian, Tim. He was always mixed up in some offbeat enterprise: hang gliding, growing hydroponic tomatoes, playing in a punk rock band. Now he was assisting with a science-fiction movie. Of course he was. I smiled.

The chapel was a typical high-ceilinged, long and narrow semi-Gothic structure. Indeed, it had lively acoustics. The chapel was adjacent to the seminary library, and I was the librarian on duty that warm March evening in Northern California. My library key also opened the chapel door.

I certainly didn't see what harm could come of it. I unlocked the door, shook hands with the two young sound guys, and went back to my library duties. Sometime later, curious, I quietly entered the rear door of the chapel and observed for a few seconds.

"Fire the retro blasters!"—that sort of cheesy thing. Nothing I heard gave me high hopes that this film would make it big. Maybe it would get picked up as a Saturday afternoon parody on TV, if they were lucky.

Later, as the guys were packing up their equipment, I asked Tim, "So what's the name of this movie going to be, so I can watch for it in the theaters?"

When he told me, I thought to myself, "Riiight . . . What a hokey title! Like I'm *ever* going to hear of a movie with such a *stupid* name as . . .

Star Wars."

Prognostication is not one of my spiritual gifts.

Fortunately, I live in a suburb with very few saber-toothed tigers.

On Listening

It was a church conference in Louisville in June, many years ago when I was young and single. One warm and humid night (obviously, Louisville in June), I stayed out late with a new friend. When we finally said good night and I returned to my hotel room, it was one in the morning. I expected to get some grief from my roommate, Greg, a married, middle-aged senior pastor of a prominent Twin Cities church.

To my great surprise, he wasn't back yet. Moments later he came through the door and, when he saw me, erupted in giggles. He was delighted to find I was still up. He had a tale he wanted to tell, if he could ever stop laughing. I immediately suspected he may have had a drink or three.

"Bill, you wouldn't believe the night that Donald and I had." Donald was another member of our Twin Cities group who had come to this national convention. At the time, he was a seminary president.

"Try me," I said, thinking of my own.

He sat on his bed. "Well, you know all the bars we pass on the way to the convention center—the ones with the big signs: 'topless and bottomless waitresses'?"

"They're hard to miss," I said.

"Well, Donald and I had been at a party. Admittedly, we'd had a couple of drinks . . ." More giggles. "And we decided it would be instructive to go inside one of those bars. So we did!"

Some of you may be shocked at the thought of a minister entering a bar of any sort, no less one advertising naked waitresses. Trust me, many pastors drink alcohol. (I don't anymore. I realized I don't need any help being stupid.) Heck, there's an old joke: Wherever you find four Episcopal priests, you will always find a fifth. And then there's this one: Jews don't recognize Jesus as the Messiah; Protestants don't recognize the pope as the head of the church; and Baptist preachers don't recognize each other in the liquor store.

Okay, back to Greg's tale: "We left the party and we walked to one of the bars and went in." More uncontrollable laughter. "Bill, the signs do not lie," he went on when he could manage it. "Topless and bottomless! The waitresses did not have *any* clothing on—not a stitch!"

"Well, I figured they weren't wearing belts," I said.

Ignoring my sarcasm, Greg continued, "Bill, you won't believe it. After just a few minutes, we actually got used to the waitresses being naked."

I pondered that.

"We asked our waitress about herself, if she had a family, where she grew up. Normal questions. But immediately she got suspicious. She said, 'Who are you guys?' She said nobody ever asks them ordinary questions about who they are as human beings.

"So I said, 'We're Presbyterian clergymen. I'm a pastor and he's the president of a theological seminary.'

"The waitress guffawed. 'Riiight! And I'm Marilyn Monroe.'

"'No, really we are,' I told her. 'Haven't you seen all the people walking by the front window going to and from the convention center with notebooks and backpacks that say *General Assembly of the Presbyterian Church?'*

"'Hmm. Yeah, I guess I have.' And then she called over all the other waitresses! We were surrounded by eight or ten naked women. 'These guys are Presbyterian pastors,' she told them.

"'Ha! Good one!' the other women scoffed. 'No, they're not. Gimme a break.'

"'No, I think they really are,' our waitress insisted.

"'Prove it,' said one of the new arrivals, looking at us.

"So we started searching our wallets for any credentials. Turns out that neither of us happened to have anything on us that said we were ministers, not even business cards. I always have a business card, but I'd given out my last one this afternoon.

"So one of the waitresses said, 'Okay, then. Name the Ten Commandments.'

"So we started to list them . . ." Greg was laughing so hard at this point I was half-afraid he was going to hurt himself. "But we—but we . . ." It was hiccups interrupting him now. "We—we could only come up with nine!"

Greg doubled over into paroxysms of laughter once again. I had to wait so long this time I almost fell asleep sitting up on my bed.

I'd had, after all, my own long, if exhilarating, night . . .

Finally recovering his breath, Greg continued. "But we stayed and talked with these women. We asked them where they had grown up, how many siblings they had, if they had kids, what they did for fun, that sort of thing. It was fascinating."

I thought back on my own evening. The conversations I'd had with my new friend out in the beautiful warm night air of June as we walked along the promenade of the Ohio River probably weren't all that different from the conversations between the pastors and the women in the bar.

More soberly now, Greg looked down at his hands as he spoke. "Gosh. They could have been our daughters . . . We listened to them talk about the challenges they've faced in their young lives, the hopes they have for their futures, or at least their kids' futures . . . We ended up chatting for two hours."

He took a deep breath, let it out, and looked up at my face. There was concern and compassion on his. "You could tell they weren't used to that," he said.

These young waitresses were used to exploitation and judgment, but these pastors treated them like human beings, like children of God.

Which they are.

MOST MEMORABLE SERMON

At various conferences and clergy gatherings, I have been privileged to hear some of the world's most acclaimed pulpit giants: Tom Long, James Forbes, Barbara Brown Taylor, and William Sloane Coffin, among others. All of them are amazingly gifted, polished, inspired, and inspiring. Coffin was an amazing wordsmith and I found myself constantly muttering under my breath, "Dang! I wish I had come up with that phrase." Taylor dances with familiar scripture passages, evoking creative insights that would never have occurred to me in a million years but seem spot on. Again, "Why didn't I think of that?"

However, the most eloquent and memorable sermon I have ever heard was delivered by a fifteen-year-old boy. My good friend and former colleague Barbara Battin tells the story:

> Matt and his family are parishioners in a former congregation of mine. Like his older brother Mark, Matt was a tall, good-looking kid, gregarious and bright, with wavy hair and an easy smile. He was quick to welcome new members to the Sunday School class. He listened carefully to other students' insights and offered his own. He could be a bit mischievous, but

never in a hurtful way. Just one of those kids you always missed when they weren't there, which was seldom. I moved to a new congregation when Matt was in fifth grade.

In middle school, Matt started to experience occasional double vision and he became even more clumsy than most boys his age as they adjust to their new size 11 feet. His worried parents brought him to their family physician, who calmly assured them, "This could be caused by any number of things. We'll run some tests."

The tests returned the worst possible diagnosis: brain tumor. Surgeons could remove only part of the tumor, and between the operation itself and the remaining tumor, Matt's cognition was significantly compromised.

A couple years later, the family came to visit me at my new church. Matt's speech was slow and he walked with a pronounced limp, but his hug was strong and long. He still had the easy smile.

I gave the family an abbreviated version of my usual tour of the building, walking slowly so Matt could keep up. His eyes were brightly taking in everything. He was delighted to see in my study a craft project he had given me years earlier, a little nativity scene he had fashioned out of clay, one of my prized possessions. When we came into the sanctuary, Matt walked straight to the chancel and then up the two steps into the pulpit.

"Preach us a sermon, Matt!" I called.

He looked out at his family and me standing in the sanctuary and at the empty pews. He raised his hand and, with his finger pointed, said simply, "God loves you . . . and you . . . and you" as his hand traveled from right to left, encompassing the whole of the sanctuary space.

Sharing a Scar

A few years ago, I glanced at the scar on my left arm and thought back to my friend, the late Lutheran pastor/ poet/artist/tour leader/author/retreat leader/hymn writer/junk sculptor Herb Brokering. Decades ago, I attended one of Brokering's seminars. At one point, he invited participants to pair off and show each other a scar on their body (if possible and appropriate, of course), then to tell the story of how they got it. It was fascinating.

I decided to try it during my sermon time a few weeks later. I had people group into twos or threes and explain the circumstances that earned them a scar. After a few moments of hesitation and finding partners and "Who's going first?" the conversation started to flow. I mean, folks *really* got into it. The noise level in the sanctuary was remarkable, with frequent peals of laughter and occasional gasps.

The two people in my group had fascinating tales, one of a horrible car accident, the other of an emergency lifesaving surgery. Mine was utterly mundane in comparison. While a teenager working in my brother's fruit and vegetable store, I had accidentally stabbed myself with a paring knife in the crook of my left arm (see "Checking Corn" elsewhere in this collection). The knife gouged out a triangular hole about the size of a nickel. You could actually see inside my arm about an inch deep—tendons and ligaments laid bare for inspection, as in an anatomy book. Amazingly, it didn't hurt a bit. I turned to the guy on my right, my high school buddy Pete, who was also checking corn, and brought my arm around to show him the hole. He glanced down and immediately swooned. Knees buckling, he sat down quickly to avoid falling. (His dad was our family physician; evidently, Pete was not going to follow in his father's footsteps.) After a few seconds, blood filled the hole and poured out of my arm, though I got it stopped in a minute or two.

I gave people only about five minutes to share their stories, and most groups were reluctant to stop.

Of course, I did get an anonymous note following the service: "Bill, don't *ever* do that again!" Huh! I have no idea what was behind that sentiment. Perhaps my exercise wasn't a normal sermon told "decently and in order"? (That's a line from the Apostle Paul that Presbyterians have informally adopted as their motto. Alas. Really, how boring is that? "Decently and in order." Sheesh.)

More likely, I think, is the exercise hit a nerve of some sort, figuratively and perhaps almost literally. It may have brought back painful memories the person didn't want to think about, much less share with a stranger. It's never my intention to cause people pain. I wish I could have asked that person for forgiveness, but that's the problem with anonymous notes. (Well, one of the problems.)

Yet most found the exercise to be interesting, at least, and perhaps even somewhat healing. Such fascinating facts we can learn about people through their scars. Who knew that Jerry ran a Tilt-A-Whirl at the State Fair, or that Sue worked in a slaughterhouse, or that Anne one summer (unwittingly) worked for the Mafia?

And think what a tale the resurrected Christ had to share about his scars . . .

But Brokering's primary point, and mine, is about the wounds we *can't* see.

I said to the congregation, "I don't think there was one adult in this sanctuary without a physical scar. But most of our truly excruciating scars are not visible; these are the emotional scars in our lives. What will we do with them?"

I shared with the congregation a story about one of the early stars of the Boston Bruins hockey team. Eddie Shore played hockey long before face masks or even helmets. As a defenseman, he was tough and fearless. He caught a lot of sticks, pucks, and fists right in the face. Over the years he received hundreds of stitches. By the time he retired, his face was a patchwork of scars.

But twenty years later, at a reunion of the club, his teammates were astounded to see Eddie's face was now completely smooth, not a scar to be seen. When asked about it, he said, "I had this skin cream. Every night I rubbed my scars with this cream, worked it in for about five minutes. Night after night. Over the years, the scars gradually got lighter and lighter. Eventually, they disappeared entirely."

But some people don't really *want* these "scars" to disappear. They pick at them; they rehearse their grievances to keep the wounds fresh. I know I had to learn this lesson the hard way after the unraveling of my first marriage. After years of painful struggling with the eroding relationship, once we finally called it quits, I thought I was ready to move on. To my surprise, I quickly found myself in a new—and wonderful—relationship. But after some time it became apparent that, in fact, I wasn't ready to move on. I needed to do some forgiving, of my ex . . . and of myself. Only then could I be whole enough to forge a new relationship of trust.

We cripple ourselves when we focus on our injuries, keeping the scars fresh. As it has frequently been said, "Resentment is like swallowing poison . . . and waiting for the other person to die."

The wisest among us know to rub on the skin cream of forgiveness.

That we might be healed.

Allow me one caveat: In the case of abuse, it is not helpful to move too quickly to forgiveness. People do well to work through those experiences with a trained therapist in order to find full and complete healing.

ON HEROES

On a shelf in my elementary school library were perhaps thirty identically bound, orange-colored books. They were just the right size for me. About nine inches tall, perhaps five or six inches wide, and just under an inch thick, they fit perfectly in my ten-year-old fingers. The font size was nice as well: not too discouragingly small, not babyishly big. The books were not brand-new, so the pages and binding felt comfy in my hands, but they weren't shabby, either. In every respect, they were for me "Goldilocks" books—just right. I was a good reader and could get through one of those books in a few hours.

Most important, of course, was what was in them. They were biographies: from Thomas Edison to Woodrow Wilson, Davy Crockett to Albert Einstein. I eagerly gobbled them up, knowing I could confidently grab any of these autumn-colored volumes off the shelf and be not only entertained, but inspired.

I don't remember for sure, but probably all the biographies were of men, and certainly they were all of white individuals, though I imagine neither of those facts struck me as unusual as a child. Maybe this was partially because I was looking in particular for role models who could show me what kind of man I could be someday. Over the years I have added Rosa Parks, Dorothy Day, Sojourner Truth, Michelle Obama, preacher and author Barbara Brown Taylor, and other women to my pantheon of heroes.

Another thing I thought about only decades later was that these were not nuanced accounts, showing any of the subject's imperfections, failures, or doubts. In these books, the larger-than-life characters marched steadily on from one accomplishment to another—with perhaps the exception of Davy Crockett, who died in vain at the Alamo. But he died valiantly and heroically. *Heroically.*

Having heroes has always been important to me. When I meet a new acquaintance, I will often ask, "Who are your heroes?" I think the answers are telling. And I would say more than half the people of whom I ask this question respond, "Hmm. I don't know that I really have any *heroes.*" To me, that's simply dumbfounding.

I might have been born this way—professors Scott T. Allison and George R. Goethals think so. Allison and Goethals have written extensively on the subject of heroes. They refer to Swiss psychiatrist Carl Jung's theory about archetypes, the idea that as humans we have inherited from our ancestors not only physical characteristics but knowledge of common experiences, knowledge that prepares us to face those experiences ourselves. Two of Jung's archetypes, write Allison and Goethals, are *heroes* and *demons*, and our innate understanding of those archetypes helps us to see the difference between right and wrong. Recent research by Canadian psychiatrists supports Jung's theory and shows that babies as young as six months old already prefer "right." When shown scenes that contained both "helper" and "hinderer" characters and asked which characters they liked best, babies nearly always chose the "helpers."

Allison and Goethals say heroes inspire us by solving problems and delivering justice; this can explain why movies about comic book superheroes are so popular. Heroes also give us hope and model positive behavior by "reveal[ing] to us the kinds of qualities we need to be in communion with others." Given all that, who wouldn't want a hero?

However, good heroes are hard to find. Throughout my life, the question "Who are my heroes?" has often become, in too many cases, "Who *were* my heroes?" Certainly many, if not all, of the people whose life stories I read as a youngster in those orange-bound biographies inspired me. Closer to home, for a long time I idolized Harmon Killebrew, the home run–slugging third baseman for the Minnesota Twins in the 1960s and 1970s. His nickname was *Killer*, but only because of his last name and his prodigious ability at bat. All reports of Killebrew at the time described him as a super-nice, unbloodthirsty guy, a warm family man with several sons, and he certainly came across that way in interviews. When, in my first foray into Little League, I was randomly given a uniform with Harmon's #3 on the back, I was ecstatic. (As it turned out, the uniform number was the *only* thing we had in common athletically.)

After he retired from baseball, it was reported Harmon and his wife were divorcing. I was incredulous and even felt a bit betrayed. I simply couldn't understand it. This was before divorce became so common and long before I was married, when I discovered just how difficult marriage could be under the best of circumstances. After my own divorce, I realized I may have been a little hard on poor old Killer.

But by then, hero-wise, I had largely moved on from baseball players. Not surprisingly, over the years I have idolized some of the pastors who have served as friends and mentors to me. One of the chief among these was the pastor of our congregation when I was in high school. I can remember sitting in church as a fifteen-year-old and being absolutely mesmerized by his sermons. (And not much other than girls was mesmerizing me in those days. He was an astonishing preacher.) When I was in tenth grade, he invited me into his office and talked to me about considering the pastorate as a vocation: a life-changing conversation.

I was shattered when, a few years later, he drowned at the age of forty-five. Then I was devastated anew. After his death, it became public knowledge he had been having an affair with at least one of our parishioners.

In the last number of years, I have learned two more of my pastoral friends and heroes were guilty of marital indiscretions. Each time I found out, I was so deeply disappointed. And angry.

I have read widely on the practice of nonviolence. It is a defining part of my life, my personal ethics, and my understanding of what it means to follow Jesus. My three greatest heroes in the field—and at one point I truly thought of each of them as heroes—are Mohandas Gandhi, Martin Luther King Jr., and John Howard Yoder, a Mennonite theologian.

For many years, King's infidelities have been widely recounted. These extramarital relationships are to me a hugely—*disappointing* is certainly too mild an adjective—stain on his legacy. More recently, it has been reported that Gandhi made it a practice to sleep naked with a number of young women, including his two grandnieces, ages eighteen and seventeen. Good grief! My newest disillusionment is discovering Yoder's abusive relationships with women, dating back decades.

I don't expect my heroes to be perfect—they might be smokers or drinkers or infrequent flossers; they might have outstanding parking tickets or library fines; they might struggle with anger and addictions and self-doubts like the rest of us—but betraying major promises and trust? Abusing one's power? For crying out loud!

Not long ago our extended family was gathered at my cousin's house following a funeral and we were reminiscing about the fun times we'd had as children at Grandpa's cabins. Grandpa had been a big part of my life as a kid, carrying four grandkids at a time on his back when we were swimming, teaching my brother and me how to fish, telling me fascinating stories of the "olden days." He modeled not only love and patience, but strong personal character and perseverance. After an early struggle with alcohol, he stayed sober for fifty years.

"You know," I mused at one point in the conversation, "something I have never been able to figure out is how Grandpa could afford to buy not one, but *two* lake cabins on the salary of a small-town police officer. I know they were small, seasonal cabins and he was notoriously cheap, but still . . ."

I expected everyone to share my puzzlement. Instead, my cousin chuckled.

"Well," he said cheerily, "he was on the take."

It took a second or two for his words to coalesce into meaning in my brain. My mouth fell open. My heart sank. My eyes blinked. Another one!

My cousin laughed at my stunned look. "Sure. The Mob ran a gambling house on the edge of town. My other grandpa was the county sheriff; he was on the take too."

This revelation knocked the stuffing out of me.

Upon later reflection, I realized these two police officials, when approached by the Mob, might not have had any good options if they wanted to keep their jobs—not to mention their *lives.* It was the Depression, after all, and each had a passel of kids.

No, I haven't had good luck with heroes in my life, other than my dad.

Maybe I have been looking in the wrong places?

I once read a story (if I could remember where, I would happily give credit) in which—as I remember it—a woman comes home from a meeting at her new church and tells her husband how much she admires one of the women in her group. The wife says she is going to try to model her life after this woman.

The husband is in the middle of building a picket fence. He says, "Well, you know, as I am making these pickets, I have an original I use as the pattern for each of the others. I don't make one and then use that as the model, and then use that latest one as the model for the next, and so on. I would no doubt get off track. I go back to the original every time, to serve as my model.

"Maybe we're best off using Jesus, the original model, as our example for living."

THE GREEN VAN

Iheard the vehicle before I saw it.

I was filling my car at the corner gas station on a beautiful spring evening. My buddy Jim was waiting in the passenger seat.

Jim and I are regular fishing and biking buddies. The son of a small-town hardware store owner, Jim is a special education teacher, working with some of the toughest kids in a challenging school district. He is amazingly patient with his students. Recognizing these kids have two and a half strikes against them, he cuts them a lot of slack.

Jim is also one of the *funniest* people I know, both intentionally and unintentionally. In high school, he was the guy who accidentally set the chemistry lab on fire and split his pants at prom. Another time, after a make-out session with his high school girlfriend at the park near her house, he couldn't get his car started when it was time to leave. He and his date had to walk to her house and sheepishly ask her dad for help. The dad quickly discovered that Jim, in his eagerness, hadn't put the car in park.

A few years ago, Jim drove up north to meet some friends and friends of friends for the weekend at the new lake home belonging to one of them. When Jim arrived, he saw seven or eight cars already there, the party in full swing. Jim let himself in and a number of folks welcomed him. He used the restroom, and then someone handed him a beer and directed him to the buffet table. He loaded up his plate and started in on the delicious food. Jim had been there for almost half an hour when he realized he hadn't seen the host yet. Or for that matter, anyone else he knew.

He was at the wrong cabin. His correct destination was two doors down.

You get the picture. This is Jim's life, most every day.

Today, he's the guy who can tell those stories with genius style and timing. He is the master of the malapropism and usually has one shirttail hanging out and perhaps his fly open. But he is a fine, fine man.

At the gas station, the thunderous noise moved off the road and into the lot. The vehicle came up behind me, not with the purr of today's late-model cars, nor the throaty rumble of a sports car or motorcycle, but with a sound from my youth, back when mufflers seemed to need replacing—at least on the ancient cars I drove—about every two or three years.

This vehicle had the classic "rattle rattle thunder clatter boom boom boom" of the old muffler commercials, with a few squeaks and belches thrown in for good measure.

The decades-old dark green minivan grumbled past and swung around to the other side of the pump ahead of me. The van bore an irregular pattern of dents, obviously from more than one accident. Tires so bald I could see their lack of tread from where I stood twenty feet away.

The van turned so I could see it head-on. I didn't want to stare, but I was curious to see who belonged to this machine. I gave a sidelong glance, expecting to see behind the wheel some pimply faced teenage boy with long, greasy hair, a contemporary version of myself at that age, a kid who felt "wheels" of any kind beat riding your skateboard or your bike or hoofin' it.

But I was wrong.

The solo occupant was a woman. As she exited the van, I gave her another quick look. Not a young woman. Not too old, either. It was hard to judge her age. Slim, in tight jeans, cowboy boots, and a gray T-shirt. Shoulder-length, straight, slightly oily brown hair. She had the wrinkles of a smoker and I could easily picture her dragging on a cigarette, though she wasn't. Of course, she *was* at a gas station.

Instead of swiping a card or beginning to pump, she headed straight into the building. Just then, my pump clicked to indicate my tank was full. I put the handle away and glanced at the screen. That made me happy. "Only thirty-nine bucks!" I thought. Usually, it was over forty. I had prepaid with a credit card, but now I was feeling kinda lucky, and I thought I'd go in and spend that extra buck on a lottery ticket.

I started toward the building, and Jim got out of the car and followed me. When I got in line, he just hung out behind me a few steps. I looked back at him. I noticed one side of his collar was flipped up. I tried to signal to him, but he didn't get it and just smiled vaguely. He was looking past me to the front of the line.

"Are you going to get something?" I asked him. "I'm gonna buy a Gopher 5. You want one?"

The van driver was right ahead of me. At the cashier's, she fished out of her right front pocket a few one-dollar bills and flipped them onto the counter. She reached into the left front pocket and found one more crumpled bill. As she counted, she carefully flattened out each one. "One. Two. Three. Four. Five. Six. Seven. Seven bucks on pump seven."

"Wow," I thought. "Seven bucks. That would fill my car forty years ago, but it hardly gets you around the block these days."

Jim didn't buy anything. While I was getting my ticket, he walked past me and headed out the door behind the woman. I followed quickly, lottery ticket in hand.

To my surprise, Jim didn't go to my car but headed instead toward the green van. I stopped by my driver's side door to watch surreptitiously; I wondered where this was going.

"Excuse me," Jim said quietly. The woman turned. "Um, here. Fill up your tank." He held out two twenties.

She blinked. Then frowned. It took a few seconds for her to understand. Then, "Oh, no, I couldn't!" she said. "That's very kind, but no." She smiled and shook her head.

"Hey," he insisted, "I had a *really great* day today. And I'd like to do this. Please. Here."

She looked at the bills. Then at his face. I don't know if she noticed his lopsided collar or not. She took a breath. Let it out. Another breath. With tears in her eyes, she slowly reached for the bills and said softly, "Thank you *so* much. You have no idea . . ." She gave him a quick hug. Then she headed back into the building to pay for a fill-up.

Only then did I open my door and get into my car. I should have known . . .

After a moment, Jim came in on the passenger side. With tears in my own eyes, I turned to my friend and asked, "Did you *really* have a great day today?"

He smiled. "I have now."

HIGH SCHOOL CLASS REUNIONS

I was one of those now increasingly rare members of the clergy who went straight from high school to college to seminary. (I don't recommend it, but I did it.) So I was only twenty-four years old when I was ordained, and by my ten-year high school reunion I had already been serving as a pastor for three years.

Our high school class was very large and most of us hadn't seen one another since graduation. Of course, one of the first questions anyone asked was, "What kind of work are you in?"

"I'm a pastor," I said to the first person who asked it of me.

My questioner threw her head back and cackled. "Ha ha ha ha! Oh, Bill, you always were so funny! No, seriously, what do you do?"

"Um." My brow furrowed; my eyes looked left, down, up, right . . . "Um, I'm . . . a pastor." I nodded to give further affirmation to the words.

Now *her* brow furrowed, and, cocking her head, she said, "Seriously?"

I nodded again.

She muttered under her breath, "Huh. Didn't see that coming." She tried once again: "You're not pulling my leg?"

Over the next few hours, that scene was repeated three or four times. I was entirely surprised and perplexed. Recently, one of my high school friends confirmed that, had there been such a category for yearbook superlatives, I would have been unanimously voted "Most likely *not* to become a pastor."

What did my classmates' reactions say about me? Or what did it say about their stereotype of pastors?

Granted, I wasn't the most blatantly pious kid in high school, spouting Bible verses or grabbing fellow students by the lapel and asking fiercely, "Are you saved?" (One of my pastor friends always answers that question with an enthusiastic "Hell, yes!") But neither was I holding up convenience stores or selling drugs or organizing keggers down by the river at which we built a blazing bonfire and sacrificed woodchucks to Satan.

Why were people *so* surprised at my vocational choice? And should I be offended? Or take it as a compliment?

In another ten years, at our class's twenty-year reunion, my childhood friend Dick and I were surveying the dance floor from the rear of the room, leaning on a railing next to each other, looking out thoughtfully at the few folks still in a dancing mood well after midnight. We talked little.

Dick and I had known each other since third grade, not the closest of friends but certainly always friendly. We had been in a few of the same classes, had both worked on my dad's farm, and had attended Sunday School together all during our growing-up years.

I don't remember if I had seen him at all since high school, so it was fun to catch up with him at this reunion. Earlier in the evening I had learned that his mom, who had been widowed that first year we met (third grade!), was widowed again but doing well. And Dick himself was doing really well—married, with a twelve-year-old son, a lucrative job he liked, and a marvelous head of hair. In fact, he was even more handsome than he'd been in high school. Looked as if he had just stepped off the cover of *GQ*.

Neither of us had brought our spouses along—fifty bucks a head, and what's more boring than going to your spouse's reunion?—so now we stood there in a comfortable silence, arms crossed on the railing, each thinking our private thoughts, until Dick started to mutter, without looking at me. Over the music I could just barely make out what he was saying.

"Bill Chadwick," he said softly.

I turned my head to face him, though he continued to stare straight ahead. "You were always so smart, all through school. You could have been anything . . . *anything*. And you became . . . a minister . . ."

The incredulity and disgust in his tone made clear the extent to which he felt I had wasted my gifts.

Dial ahead another five years: Dick was there again, looking delighted to spot me as I entered the ballroom. He hadn't lost a single hair off his head. A few on the temple were gray, but that only served to make him look even *more* handsome and distinguished. (Good thing I'm not one of those shallow people who care about looks.)

But not all was well. Dick hurried over, a huge smile on his face and arms spread wide for a big hug. (Five years earlier, I remembered, it had definitely been a handshake.) He eagerly pumped me for information on my family and what was going on in my life. He was excited to hear I had recently moved to a new congregation, and probed for detailed information about the church. Clearly he was sincerely curious, and I was puzzled. Neither of us mentioned his quiet mutterings of five years before.

Finally, he let me turn the tables and ask him about *his* life. "Bill," he said, "it's been pretty rough. Went through a divorce. Really horrible, especially for my son . . ."

Ah . . . so *that's* why my vocational choice no longer filled him with contempt and dismay. He had been confronted with some big issues in life and was hungrier for deeper meaning than he had been five years earlier, when life was rolling smoothly along.

We've kept in touch, and a few years ago he asked me to officiate at his mom's funeral, knowing I had something important to say about the meaning of life. And death.

I look forward to seeing him at the next reunion.

ON MOTORCYCLES

A story is told about a man who decided to buy a motorcycle. At the dealership, he was spied by a salesperson who immediately started extolling the racy virtues of the particular model the man was eyeing. "Oh, you'll love this. This baby has a throaty growl and incredible acceleration that really gets your blood pumping . . . What line of work are you in?"

When the potential customer replied that he was a pastor, the salesperson immediately shifted to emphasizing the bike's safety features and sensible gas mileage.

That story really fries my potatoes.

We pastors hate to be thought of as boring and timid. In fact, any minister worth her salt trying to be faithful to Jesus will invariably be involved in challenging and sometimes dangerous activities. The key line there is *faithful to Jesus*—a person who, you will recall, did not die of old age as he rocked his grandchildren.

In living out my faith, I have several times felt my life in jeopardy while mediating in domestic disputes; plus, during peaceful protests against various wars, I have been jailed twice and maced once.

But that is nothing compared to the thousands of clergy who have been martyred for their faithfulness. I'm not just talking about persecution during the early days of the Church.

An estimated three thousand clergy died in Poland at the hands of the Nazis.

Martin Luther King Jr. became a prominent civil rights leader because of his allegiance to Jesus. The Civil Rights Memorial in Montgomery, Alabama, lists forty martyrs killed during the civil rights struggles between 1954 and 1968. Three of those were pastors, and a fourth was a seminarian.

Father Stanley Rother, a Roman Catholic priest, was martyred in Guatemala in 1981 for speaking up for the poor. All told, dozens of priests and nuns were killed in Central America during the 1980s as they stood up on behalf of human rights and justice.

Among the nine people murdered in 2015 by a white supremacist in the Emanuel African Methodist Episcopal Church in Charleston, South Carolina—a prominent congregation long involved in civil rights—was the Reverend Clementa C. Pinckney, the church pastor and a prominent state senator. The worshipers had invited the shooter to study the Bible with them after he entered the church.

Father Joseph Désiré Angbabata was killed on March 21, 2018, for helping refugees in the Central African Republic.

Many Christians in Nigeria have been victims of violence, dating back to the year 2000 and continuing today, including dozens of pastors and their families.

In Mexico over the past ten years, more than a dozen priests have been killed by organized crime for speaking out against the drug cartels.

The list goes on.

That clergy are persecuted and even killed should not be a surprise. The values and principles Christians are called to espouse often run counter to powerful political or financial interests in their countries or regions. Remember, Jesus died as a political criminal.

In a sermon on Graduation Sunday a few years ago, I challenged the graduates to do three things. I don't remember the first two—neither does anyone else—but the last one was "Go to jail." I gave many examples of those who have taken this risk for their beliefs: from Rosa Parks to Daniel and Philip Berrigan to Dorothy Day. Even in a democracy like the US, faithfully following Jesus *should* get one crossways with political authorities. (Interesting word: *crossways*.)

So if a pastor wants to blow off some steam on a motorcycle, let her!

And make sure it's loud and fast.

To Know the Whole Story

There are many passages of scripture that make any thinking person feel uncomfortable, if not downright outraged. One verse that used to make me throw my hands up in despair was that line from the Sermon on the Mount in which Jesus commands his followers to "Be perfect, as your Father in Heaven is perfect (Matthew 5:48)."

Be perfect? Perfect! Seriously? That ain't happenin'. Not for any of us.

I have good news for us. That's not a very good translation. Recent scholarship has noted the sentence should better read "Be *compassionate*, as your Father in Heaven is compassionate." And that Greek word translated as *compassionate* shares the same root as the word for *womb*. Isn't that a powerful picture? Be compassionate as you would be toward the one who came from your womb. Perfection? No. Compassion I can do.

Especially if I know the whole story.

When you stand in front of a typical middle-class congregation of worshippers and look out at their well-scrubbed, smiling faces, it wouldn't be hard to imagine this is a group of folks who have it all together. Good jobs, nice homes, loving family members . . . life is good. And easy.

It wouldn't be hard to imagine all that *unless* . . . one is their pastor. Then one knows the heartache in each and every family unit—the grandmother with dementia, the father who cannot keep a job, the spouse who is unfaithful, the teenage daughter hospitalized with an eating disorder; or the recent cancer diagnosis, the struggles with addiction, the anxiety and depression.

Life is hard. For everybody. If, for a particular family, it isn't hard at the moment, it *was* hard last month, or it *will* be next month. That's just the way life is.

She had a gentle voice and a lovely face. I had recently come to this particular congregation as pastor, and Marian was one of the key leaders of the church. A few years older than I, married, with four delightful children. I immediately took a liking to her.

Within a year, however, things started to change. I proposed a modification to our wedding policy, which she adamantly opposed. My Christmas Eve sermon, which had garnered many positive comments, got this response from her during a council meeting: "I didn't like it *at all*." I was a bit hurt, though I had to admire her brutal honesty.

Now, I make mistakes on a regular basis. And it's certainly all right to disagree with me, perfectly legitimate to not appreciate a particular sermon. Heck, even *I* don't like some of my sermons. More than once I have found myself thinking, "Maybe it's time to go back to the farm."

But soon Marian's criticism seemed like a knee-jerk reaction. Anything and everything I said or did, she was against it. I commented to my wife, "I feel like if I said, 'The sun rises in the east,' Marian would say, 'No, it doesn't. You're wrong. It rises in the north!'"

I couldn't figure it out. I had not run into anything quite like this in my dozen years in ministry. I forced myself to act normally toward Marian, but I admit I did not like her anymore. At all. Her once-lovely face now usually wore a sour expression. Or maybe it just seemed that way to me.

After a few years, Marian and her husband stopped coming to church. As you can imagine, this was a relief. But it also made me sad. I was disappointed we hadn't been able to work through our differences.

Sometime later, I discovered two things about Marian. One was that her mother had suffered greatly from mental illness, and this had, of course, significantly colored Marian's childhood. In fact, her mother had died by suicide on Marian's twelfth birthday.

I also found out that during the time Marian had been persecuting me, there were significant, horribly painful issues happening within her family.

This knowledge completely changed my attitude toward her. I felt quite differently about the way she'd treated me. I thought, "Well, that wasn't any fun, but I'm glad she took it out on me rather than yell at her kids or kick her dog."

It really helps to know the whole story.

A dozen years later, we had moved to a new church and a new community. Our children were all old enough to be in school, we had a big yard, and the kids and my spouse thought it would be great fun to get a puppy. Knowing how much work dogs are, and who would be doing the work, I said, "Over my dead body! If a dog moves into this house, I am moving out."

"We'll miss you," they said.

Eddie was about two months old, a "mixed breed" (polite language for *mutt*) rescue dog, fluffy, yellow and white, with the double coat and curled tail of a husky. If we were going to have a dog, I thought, let's do it right and make sure it's well trained. So we forked over pretty big bucks to have a professional dog trainer come to our house and instruct the dog, and, more importantly, us.

With results that were mixed at best.

We humans had trouble understanding the trainer's very British accent; maybe Eddie did too. After all, Eddie was originally from Kentucky.

During the final session, the trainer said, "I have *never* before had a dog I couldn't train to heel." Hmm. We couldn't figure out—and eight years later still haven't—if Eddie was really dumb or really smart. I suppose it was possible he *chose* not to heel, or follow most other commands, just because he simply didn't feel like it.

Eddie looked like a stuffed animal. His plush coat just begged to be petted. However, Eddie didn't usually like to be petted and would walk away from you while you were trying to do so. "Seriously? You have one job around here," I would shout at him in exasperation. "He's like a fifty-pound cat," I would mutter.

While Eddie didn't like humans much, he *loved* other dogs. He pulled eagerly on his leash (ignoring all commands to "heel") to rush up to a fellow canine and participate in the requisite and disgusting sniffing rituals. For some reason, he was a bit skittish around little dogs, but he adored all of the big ones.

Until one day. (Now note this is one of the very few personal stories in which I look good. Most of them are more along the lines of "Learn from my bad example.") My wife was walking Eddie in the neighborhood when a large black-and-brown dog attacked him. My wife and the other dog's owner were ultimately able to separate the two, and Eddie was not badly hurt, but he was traumatized. Plus, he became a racist. He still loved all dogs . . . *except* large black-and-brown ones. He would go berserk whenever he spotted one.

One winter day, my wife took Eddie out to the front yard to do his business in the snow. Around the corner came a young man walking his dog. A black-and-brown dog. Not the same dog that had attacked Eddie a few months earlier, but just as big.

Eddie lunged against his leash. He barked and growled and pulled so hard he freed himself from my wife's grip. In three bounds Eddie was on this other dog in a frenzy, biting, snarling, and fighting back when the other dog proved to be equally ferocious.

My wife stood where she was, frozen in horror. Then she commanded in her loudest and firmest voice, "Eddie, come! Eddie! Come!"

She might as well have commanded Eddie to recite the Gettysburg Address. The young man was also yelling. He yanked on his own dog's leash and kicked at Eddie. Seeing all this through the living room window, I raced outside in my bare feet and was somehow able to grab Eddie's leash. The other owner and I separated the two dogs, and I was hugely relieved when it became clear that neither was hurt.

As I dragged Eddie toward our house, I said, "I'm so, so sorry."

I looked at the young man, who was about thirty, short, and stocky. He was backing up with his own barking dog, his face twisted with rage. Before I could explain why Eddie hated/feared black-and-brown dogs, he yelled, "You G—— D—— liberals!" He was so angry he was spewing spittle when he added, "I oughta shoot that f——ing dog like they do in Iraq!"

Then he hurried down the street. My wife and I stood in stunned silence. (The "liberals" comment no doubt stemmed from the campaign signs we sometimes had in our yard and the "peace" sign permanently in our front window.)

That night around the supper table, my wife and I shared the story with our three teenage children. They were outraged and expressed their loathing toward the owner of the other dog.

I said, "Well, I could have done without the profanity and the name-calling, but it *was* our fault. He was scared! He was just out for a stroll with his dog when Eddie attacked. Besides," I added, thinking back to my experience with Marian and others like her, "we don't know what kind of day he was having."

Our kids were unconvinced and cut him no slack.

A couple of months later, I was walking Eddie through the neighborhood when around a curve I saw, across the street and walking in our direction, a young man and a dog. All too soon I could see the young man was short and stocky, and the dog was brown and black.

My first impulse was to turn around and get Eddie out of there, but I decided I would once again apologize and explain why Eddie had acted the way he did.

As we got closer, the two dogs, of course, started barking and pulling, trying to get at each other's throats. But both the young man and I held firm. I called out across the street, "Hey, again, I'm so sorry about Eddie attacking your dog."

As I was going on to further explain—"The problem is, he was attacked by a black-and-brown dog and now he's afraid of all of them"—I realized the young man was doing the same thing.

"No, *I* apologize," he said. "I shouldn't have said that. My mom says Eddie is a good dog. I just lost my temper . . . You see, that morning I had gotten word that my buddy had been killed in Iraq."

If we could know the full history of a person, if we could truly get inside their skin, feel what they have experienced, then we could understand their actions, no matter how seemingly incomprehensible, or even reprehensible.

Listen to this story of a childhood. Shortly before the time of his birth, two tragedies struck the family: the father died and the boy's older brother, twelve years old, died of cancer. In a state of much distress, the mother attempted suicide. Before the child's birth, she would pull out clumps of her hair and pummel her pregnant abdomen with her fists. She is quoted in a February 1991 *Wall Street Journal* article as having said she did not want this baby, saying, "After losing my husband and child, what good can this baby do me?" Three years later his mother remarried. The stepfather horribly beat the boy for years. At ten, the lad was sent to live with an uncle who indoctrinated him in the ways of a violent revolutionary political party.

Could Saddam Hussein have turned out any other way?

I'm not saying we let abusers and murderers go free. They need to be incarcerated so we do not perpetuate the cycle of violence. What I am saying is if we know the whole story, then even the most bizarre and violent behavior becomes at least somewhat understandable.

A few years ago, I sat down to breakfast with a young man who had served in the US military in Afghanistan. Our conversation was fascinating. Among many other things, we talked about vocational opportunities for Afghan men.

He told me farmers can make ten times as much money growing poppies for opium as they can growing vegetables. Not surprising.

What was news to me was this: If you are the son of a farmer in Afghanistan but not the oldest son, who inherits the land, you essentially have three choices of employment. You can join the police, the military, or the Taliban. Guess which provides you with the least likelihood of being killed? The Taliban. And which pays the highest wage? The Taliban.

All behavior is understandable when we know what is behind it.

I think that's why God is so good at this forgiveness business. She always knows the whole story.

May we be compassionate, as our God in Heaven is compassionate.

Acknowledgments

I have to begin with a hearty thank-you to my dad for his stories of the good ol' days, many of which we kids heard as we rode along with him in the '49 Ford truck on his delivery of farm produce. Others came when we were gathered around the fireplace at home. My siblings and I were somehow wise enough to appreciate the stories even at the time. What we would give to hear another!

Writing teachers and coaches—Elizabeth Andrew, Cheri Johnson, and Rachel Moritz—took my straw and occasionally spun it into gold, or at the very least a significant improvement over straw. Despite having been a writer of sermons for decades, I knew virtually nothing about writing a book. I was used to writing fast. Come Sunday I was done. Period. On to the next sermon. But they taught me the value and necessity of rewriting. And sitting with a piece. And then rewriting again. And again. Elizabeth said, "Sometimes a writer doesn't know what a piece is about until the third or fourth time through," and I found that to be true.

Thanks to two of my beloved congregations, St. Luke Presbyterian in Minnetonka, Minnesota, and Oak Grove Presbyterian in Bloomington, Minnesota, for the gift of sabbaticals, during which most of the writing took place. And to my sister-in-law and brother-in-law, Lynn and Rich Voelbel, for graciously sharing their cabin for uninterrupted writing.

A huge thank-you to Arlene and Joe Jullie for their cheerleading and supporting the recording of this book.

Dear friend Margie O'Loughlin was not only the patient photographer, but a wonderful encourager. I have such gratitude for all my partners at Beaver's Pond Press, especially Project Manager Laurie Herrmann and Designer Jim Handrigan.

And, of course, abundant thanks to my cherished children and patient spouse, who gave me time and encouragement and provided me with much of the raw material.